"With grace, honesty, humor, and an uncanny ability to braid her story seamlessly with biblical examples, Jamie Sumner shares a deeply personal, tender, and yet arduous journey into motherhood. Hers isn't a straight, freshly paved path. No. There are pot holes and U-turns, road blocks and red lights. But these obstacles are only part of the story. *Unbound* is really about yielding to a plan different than one's own. It's about yielding to a God who knows us and loves us, and leads us on the path everlasting. This isn't just Jamie's story. It's everyone's. I cried at the end of this book."

—Gillian Marchenko, author of *Sun Shine Down: A Memoir* and *Still Life: A Memoir of Living Fully with Depression*

"Eloquent and inspiring, *Unbound* connects modern-day motherhood with the stories of women found throughout scripture. Jamie Sumner peels back the outer layers of her own journey though infertility and raising children with special needs, and exposes heart-warming and relatable accounts of hardship, perseverance, and growth. Sumner sings truth and encouragement, grounded in biblical verses, reminding us all to stay present through this beautifully complicated season of raising tiny humans."

—Kristin M. Helms, author of *From Boardroom to Baby: A Roadmap for Career Women Transitioning to Stay-at-Home Moms*

"Jamie Sumner approaches the ups and downs of motherhood with honesty and wit, making us all feel a little better about the job we're doing . . . while at the same time inspiring us through the fact that we're not alone. Women through history—from the ancient Old Testament to now—have all struggled to find the balance of their identity in Christ and as for our souls."

ue, co-author of *The Essential Five: -Up Girl's Handbook for Everything*

"Jamie Sumner is a writer of words women need to read. Women will joyfully cheer that in *Unbound*, Sumner talks about the little-discussed realities of infertility and miscarriage. She then takes us forward through the getting and the appreciation of motherhood. Brilliantly, she ties together her stories with those of biblical females and makes all of us moms find freedom from our unrealistic expectations as we claim our God-given strength. This is a joy of a read."

—Sarah Philpott, PhD, author of *Loved Baby: 31 Devotions Helping You Grieve and Cherish Your Child After Pregnancy Loss* (connect with her at allamericanmom.net)

"As a woman who's struggled with infertility for over four years, I felt such a connection to Jamie and her story through reading this work of love. There's something crazy about this world of trying-to-conceive that no one tells you: the friendships you make through sharing the mutually exhaustive trials and tribulations of infertility. I believe there's a reason for everything in my heart of hearts, and as I come off my second FET with no bump yet to show, I know there is a reason God brought me to Jamie and this book—to remind me, as she so eloquently puts it, 'God has a plan. He's already stitched it together for you and it is masterful and, lucky for all of us, already complete.'

"So, to my fellow #ttcsisters, if you're looking for a friend on this bumpy ride, I would definitely recommend cozying up with *Unbound* to laugh, cry, and seek that friend who gets you during this trying time. You are not alone, and Jamie will remind you of that!"

—Elizabeth Shaw, MS, RDN, CLT, fertility nutrition expert, writer for *Self* and *Fit Pregnancy*, founder of BumpstoBaby.com, co-author of *Fertility Foods Cookbook*

Unbound

Finding Freedom from Unrealistic Expectations of Motherhood

Jamie Sumner

New York   Nashville

FaithWords
Hachette Book Group
1290 Avenue of the Americas, New York, NY 10104
faithwords.com
twitter.com/faithwords

Scriptures taken from the Holy Bible, New International Version®, NIV®. Copyright © 1973, 1978, 1984, 2011 by Biblica, Inc.™ Used by permission of Zondervan. All rights reserved worldwide. www.zondervan.com. The "NIV" and "New International Version" are trademarks registered in the United States Patent and Trademark Office by Biblica, Inc.™

First Edition: April 2018

FaithWords is a division of Hachette Book Group, Inc. The FaithWords name and logo are trademarks of Hachette Book Group, Inc.

The publisher is not responsible for websites (or their content) that are not owned by the publisher.

The Hachette Speakers Bureau provides a wide range of authors for speaking events. To find out more, go to www.hachettespeakersbureau.com or call (866) 376-6591.

Library of Congress Cataloging-in-Publication Data has been applied for.

ISBNs: 978-1-5460-3198-7 (trade paperback), 978-1-5460-3196-3 (ebook)

Printed in the United States of America

LSC-C

10 9 8 7 6 5 4 3 2 1

For Charlie.
You are my sunshine.
I will always play the music loud for you.

Contents

Contents

The Getting

The Appreciating

Introduction

"The Honeymoon" and Paul's Benediction

What can I say about the honeymoon phase, other than it should be bliss. *Should be.* I so wish someone had encouraged me to take a breather before embarking on the baby journey. Although to be totally honest, if a neighbor or friend had told me to enjoy that newly wedded era in a well-meaning over-the-fence conversation, I wouldn't have listened. Stay on your side and I'll stay on mine. There are too many voices from too many sides offering advice at that stage of life. Your married friends tell you to hold off and enjoy the freedom. Meanwhile, parents and anyone over fifty whisper, "So when are we going to have some little ones running around?" wink wink, nudge nudge. It's advice overload. Soon enough, the system shuts down and reboots, wiped clean of anything but your own agenda.

I was twenty-five when I got married and not ready for the question about kids or the answer that would come years later. However, as a girl with a zesty obsessive-compulsive bent, I let the idea of babies infiltrate the early days of wedded bliss. I had one foot on the baby train even on the honeymoon. The Mai Tai cocktail hour had nothing on the future bliss that I thought was motherhood. It was the life upgrade I'd been waiting for. Cue the imaginary shopping at Pottery Barn Kids. I knew I wasn't ready yet. "We" weren't ready yet, but I'm not great at treading water. Sink or swim. "Be still and know that I am God" (Psalm 46:10) is my most underlined verse in the Bible for a reason. This, if you ask my husband, Jody, is a continual source of both excitement and irritation in our marriage. I want to live in the moment, but deep down, I feel like I can do it better if I'm also allowed to plan ahead just a bit. Cultivate my spontaneity, like Mario busting through walls and aiming for the next magical coin.

God shows himself best in hindsight. I wish I had enjoyed those early years of marriage when I was learning how to be a grown-up living with another grown-up. It was a season ripe for learning. We ate large quantities of peanut butter and jelly on Wheat Thins, because who has time for knives and bread those first few years? We saw a lot of live music, eardrums buzzing for days. We slept in and went out to our favorite local coffee shop, sitting in the sun on their porch, sipping Americanos and competing at crossword puzzles. We learned how to work full-time jobs and still be nice to each other. We combined finances and CDs (back when those still existed) and furniture as best we could. We met up with friends and traveled aimlessly as only unencumbered twenty-somethings could. And we joined a Sunday school class for those newly married, admission to a club of other confused and fumbling people with an excess of unreturnable wedding gifts. God bless the married veterans who took us all on for that season of life. Because despite all of these newly married happenings, I could not stop thinking about the next "happening." After two years the honeymoon finally ended and the "process of trying" began.

Here's what got that train in motion. Jody and I were driving back from his parents' home a few hours away, where we had gone to tailgate and attend a football game. His was a college town, do or die by school pride. Autumn was just beginning to make itself known—the time of year all the ladies whip out scarves and boots, despite the weather, and the men live the life of fantasy football stats, despite reality and limited funds. This, for me as a high school English teacher, has always been the season of anticipation. Pens are still full of ink. Post-its reach towering heights, a spectrum of possibility. And I'm finding the different rhythm with each of my classes. It's soothing when the blinding light of summer mellows and the first round of essays and football games begin.

Jody drove. And while I graded with feet propped up, I felt it in a corner of my mind, a gentle tapping. The conversation we had only just tiptoed around had finally come knocking, like a Girl Scout with cookies.

Jody is a warmer-upper. He's the kind of man who likes to get used to an idea, see it from every angle, read all the reviews, before tentatively clicking "Purchase." I knew this by now and had already done the priming: "Can you believe we've already been married two years?" I'd say over a dinner that involved actual utensils, just a tiny question slipped in every now and then to make sure he noted where we fell on the timeline. "Did you know so-and-so is pregnant?" I'd say when we passed the Pottery Barn Kids at the mall, tiny little nautical quilts hanging in the window. Hear me when I say I did try to temper my expectations. I didn't want him to think I was desperate. I can be a tsunami of need if I'm not careful.

But on this particular fall day, I felt the moment ripen. And so, we had "the talk." He later admitted I was not the cool cat I thought I was. I scream loudly, even in the pauses. Isn't that always the way in marriage and with God? We're never as sly as we think we are.

Wilco was on the radio and our team had won and we had made good time getting home. All was well. I plunged in: "When do you think we should start trying?" And before he could answer, I added, "You know, if we started now, we could have the baby in the summer and I wouldn't have to take time off from work." This was to prove I was being practical, had thought it through, and was not the crazy lady who already, and secretly, owned a baby-naming book. He let a moment pass and I stopped breathing, afraid to break the moment and watch it tilt away from me. But as we pulled into our driveway on that Sunday afternoon, he parked the car, nodded, still not quite looking at me, and said, "Now sounds like the perfect time."

And then we had a baby.

Oh wait, no, that's someone else's story. Ours is much longer.

———————

When Paul was ending his letter to the Thessalonians, he did what he always did and gave them one last nugget of wisdom as a farewell. A benediction: Adieu, my good men and women, and remember, always do X and don't forget Y. It's the parting instructions as the students rush out the door, the final reminder before real life resumes. Paul told those Thessalonians, "Be joyful always; pray continually; give thanks in all circumstances, for this is God's will for you in Christ Jesus" (1 Thessalonians 5:16). I like this reminder. It feels like a task, and I'm good at those. This is how I approached motherhood. I would be thankful for all the bumps along the road and would present all my anxiety to God, assuming the bumps were small and the anxiety only the two-minute wait for the pregnancy test.

I had been on birth control pills for over a decade due to irregular periods. Yet somehow, I expected to be functioning like a well-oiled 1950s baby-making machine. I wanted my 2.4 kids and I wanted them now!

When a few months went by and nothing happened, a mild panic set in, like a low-grade fever. I tried to live joyfully in the moment. I lit lavender-scented candles and took the dog on long walks and thanked God for the ability to sleep in on a Saturday and have a glass of wine with dinner. And I really tried not to Google herbal remedies for encouraging menstruation and femoral massage. I aimed for giving thanks "in all circumstances," hoping to nail that lesson so we could move on. Level 2 in the video game of life. But God is not Player 1, and you are not Player 2. He is the creator. He doesn't gamble with your feelings and He doesn't barter, as much as we wish He did.

Hindsight would show me that staying in the present was the only way to stay sane in those early years, and all the ones to follow. It's the lesson I needed to learn even as we sat on the black sands in Saint Lucia on our honeymoon, and the lesson I needed to learn when it was September and I began the countdown to Christmas, and it's the lesson I still need to learn when I wish myself past this house, this hair length, this episode of *This Is Us*.

I don't have to love the moment I'm in . . . I'm too much a realist for that, but God does call me to be present in it. That is my prayer and benediction for you as you juggle your expectations of motherhood. As disorienting as it might seem, may you remember to stay present, be still, and take notice of the moment you are in. That is what the women of the Bible learned to do in each of their impossible situations, and that is why they are included in each chapter of this book. I hope you will learn from their stories and mine. You do not need to "do" anything. Just be willing to be. That is, for better or worse, what trusting God looks like most of the time. It's a lot of waiting and seeing and then taking the step He lights up . . . even if it's tiny, even if it's a step backward over a cliff into a new territory. Because ultimately, He sees forward and backward and always will lead you in the right direction.

The Wanting

Chapter 1

"The Trying" and Hannah

It felt comfortable stepping into the gently flowing river of couples who were trying to conceive. Many of our friends already had babies and were on to their second or third, like a round of drinks. We felt like part of the gang, *Cheers*-style, where everybody knows your name—and your business. But I didn't mind the questions at first. I wanted to talk about cycle length and ovulation days and the days that Jody needed to move heaven and earth to avoid being sent out of town for work so that this baby magic could happen. A few friends even started pawning off their kids' outgrown shoes, baby hats, Melissa and Doug puzzles. It was like we had cruised right into pregnancy and babyhood without the conception part. Because that's what happens. People take it for granted that you'll get pregnant. I mean, if teenagers can look at each other and make a baby, and movies like *Knocked Up* and *Nine Months* exist, then surely a nice Christian married couple can follow in good stead.

But if there was a secret to this particular parlor trick, we weren't in on it. No amount of smoke and mirrors was going to make that pregnancy test show two lines. This was the part I did not share with friends. I barely spoke it to myself.

You remember Hannah, mother of Samuel, right? She was married to a man named Elkanah, who never gets much screen time in this story. Elkanah was also married to Peninnah. She was a vending machine of fertility. She had lots and lots of babies. Hannah had none. Peninnah was the kid in the cafeteria who always had the best lunch, the fun stuff, like psychedelic Goldfish and two desserts. That's also the kid who always lines it all up on the table so everyone can see but no one can touch. Peninnah tormented Hannah year after year, the bully in the lunchroom. Every time Hannah walked into the house, Penninah "kept provoking her in order to irritate her" (1 Samuel 1:6) and brought her to tears, prodding her into more of a weepy hormonal mess than she already was.

Poor Hannah, she, too, probably knew that stress was bad for conception. There's nothing less conducive to a calm uterus than stressing about stress. Elkanah wasn't much help. "Why are you weeping?" he asked her. "Why don't you eat? Why are you downhearted? Don't I mean more to you than ten sons?" (1 Samuel 1:8). He could not understand why she wouldn't just be happy with him, sans kids. "Aren't I good enough?"

Yes and no, I wanted to say every time Jody and I had a variation of the same conversation. How do you explain a part of you that can be filled only by a child? Hannah couldn't explain it; but she took her wishes to the Lord and prayed, "If you would only look upon your servant's misery and remember me, and not forget your servant but give her a son, then I will give him to the Lord for all the days of his life" (I Samuel 1:11). We all know how that went. Baby Samuel.

In that first year, I thought about Hannah often. I wept and prayed. I prayed and wept. I thought up deals in my head:

The Wanting

Dear God, please just let me ovulate this month and I'll rest and spend more time reading Scripture and do my daily gratitudes. Dear God, please let this cycle be a normal twenty-eight days and I'll make a home-cooked meal every night and not skip community group at church. Dear God . . . I offered bargain after bargain. I prayed with my hands on the Bible as if it were a Ouija board. Please spell out B-A-B-Y. And with every month that passed without success, I slowly lowered the dimmer switch on my view of God's goodness. Clearly, He didn't care whether I got pregnant or not. Clearly, I wasn't that important to Him. I wasn't Hannah, or any of the teeming millions of pregnant women who suddenly seemed to live within a five-mile radius of my house. This menacing train of thought made a station stop in every part of my life. I issued demerits to my high school students one second after the bell rang to begin class. Grace period was for elementary school. I refused to allow Jody to have any issues other than conception. Trouble with work? I did not even pretend to listen, because it seemed so small in comparison. Even the poor dog was too needy. "What, you need to go out again?"

The only surprising thing about this time was that I was not perpetually depressed. I had my ups as well as downs. I am, if nothing else, a roller coaster of emotions. I will always spend too long trying to pick an emoticon. During the long wait, I still laughed when we watched *The Office* and I still took the dog for walks. I still lost myself in teaching *The Catcher in the Rye* and *Lord of the Flies*, kids gone wild, a Freudian curriculum slip. But it all felt a bit hollow. Or I was hollow and none of it was doing the trick to fill me up. Jody did not know whom he would be coming home to at the end of each day.

He waited, watching my face as he walked in the door before assembling his own. I do not envy him those few seconds.

The thing I didn't realize at the time was that a baby wasn't going to fill that hollowness either, or at least not in the eternally satisfying way that you picture getting the thing you currently want. If anything worked that way, commercialism would be out the window. We buy new clothes and new phones in the hope that the satisfaction will stick like a super-sized value meal. Somehow, I had tacked the "baby" label on to "fulfillment" and could not see a Plan B. That was my one heart's desire. Period.

Though I knew Hannah's story well during that time, the thing about her situation that I did not care to notice until years later was the order of events. She didn't ask God for a baby, have a baby, and then walk away happy. She asked God for a baby and *immediately* walked away happy: "Her face was no longer downcast" (1 Samuel 1:18). This was before the positive pregnancy test, my friends, before she got the "yes" to her request. She found a peace just in the naming of her desire and holding it up for God to inspect. She did not know the end point of her path, but she felt better in letting someone else walk it for a while, because now it was out of her hands.

Does that get you the way it gets me? Placing my hopes, desires, needs in God's hands has never been my strong suit, or even a middling one. I always feel like there is a part of my life's journey that is still under my operating instructions. Desperate to control my way to motherhood, I was playing life's version of the Claw, the arcade game where you steer the dangling robot hand, cross your fingers, and aim for the biggest stuffed duck. If I could just maneuver my life a tad up and to the left, I'd be able to win the prize. Hannah's lesson was not to guess God's price for a baby and offer it, but to let it go and walk away from the levers. She knew there was someone whose plan was greater than hers, and who would answer her prayer in His time and in His way.

But for me, in that first year, as "It's a girl/boy" Facebook posts increased exponentially as if someone were buying up Google Ads for babies, and I trudged along empty, I had not yet learned the lesson of unburdening. It was maddening to even consider. Instead, I took matters into my own hands. I went to see my general practitioner, who sent me to an OB-GYN, who put me on Clomid, the standard Phase 1 baby-inducing medicine. Here, take these pills; come back for a blood test. We'll see if you're ovulating and then get that baby on board. It usually works like a charm. Three months of this with no success and I became one of those "difficult cases." They referred me to a RE (reproductive endocrinologist), saying I was outside the realm of their expertise. How terrifying. These people had gone to medical school and had helped thousands of women get and stay pregnant, yet I was beyond their abilities. But also, how exciting: a new option I hadn't thought of. This RE person would fix it all! She would hold the litmus test to determine what I'd been missing all along. I couldn't give the control to God, but giving it to an expert whom I could see and touch and hear explain all the ways she was going to fix it seemed easy. I became excited and hopeful again. *This last year was really just a bump in the road*, I told myself. *I'm so glad I weathered that so well*, I said, even as the water pooled around my psyche. The power of delusion is strong in me.

The doctor's office tower was a nondescript concrete building downtown surrounded by other nondescript medical complexes. It was all a gray maze of one-way streets and no-parking signs and the elderly in wheelchairs waiting at intersections like abandoned shopping carts while police officers directed traffic. Jody and I drove together and talked of anything but what was coming. It was the one and only time I actually turned up the volume to *Car Talk* on NPR. It was autumn again. Another new beginning.

The office was on the top floor, and the elevator opened directly in front of the fertility clinic's doors, their glass windows frosted and etched with the silhouette of a baby. It looked peaceful, asleep, waiting for the stork to drop it into my cage. Despite the fact that I had filled out reams of paperwork before the appointment, I had no clue how this was going to play out. After signing in, we received our matching wristbands. Jody's stuck to his arm hair. It would happen each time we returned to the clinic and is the reason he still has a bald spot on his wrist.

And then, the awkward wait with all the other empty vessels. No magazine could have been engaging enough to make that wait go any faster. I would later come to learn the Rules of the Waiting Room: (1) No eye contact. Ever. (2) No small talk (that's what support groups are for). (3) No talking loudly to your partner (we don't want to know if you are in love or fighting or your plans for lunch). (4) And absolutely no children (this is an actual rule posted at the front desk). Please don't parade your progeny in front of the needy.

That first initial meeting went smoothly. We discussed and dismissed Clomid (silly useless drug) in favor of stronger, more precise remedies. I would take a different oral medication to induce ovulation, and if that didn't work, try injections, and if that didn't work, try injections plus IUIs (intrauterine insemination), and if three to six cycles of those didn't work, we would move on to the biggie: IVF (in vitro fertilization). So many ifs! But that was, of course, a last resort, our petite and precise RE amended. We also skirted over the costs of these methods. Doctors do not deal in numbers other than mls and ccs. We would not find out until later that insurance and barrenness weren't friendly in our state. They did not play well together. But before all that, our RE said, standing and smoothing her skirt, "Let's just do some blood tests to determine the root cause of the infertility." Because this was now my initial diagnosis. I was "infertile." Truth: It felt good to name it. Slap a label on me and mark for resale. I was ready to move on. My land was parched, and now the doctor could begin the process of irrigation.

We left that day with Band-Aids on our arms and just a small skip in our step. I love a plan, and this plan had so many parts, and most likely we wouldn't even need most of those parts, but it was so nice to know that they were there just in case and isn't the sky a lovely blue today? Jody was sweet and calm and tentative in his hopes (the rational winner in our partnership), but because he gets me, he let me revel in this burst of sanguinity. Our journey to parenthood would look a bit different than others, but hey, at least we'd get there.

Remember Hannah? Yeah, I forgot about her too. Her approach of waiting in peacefulness, stillness, and joy sat with me about as well as late-night Taco Bell. I kept burping up her passivity. She was clearly not a kindred spirit. Isn't it so easy to parcel out the parts of the Bible you don't need? What was vital one day was forgotten the next. Hannah got lost in a swirl of test results and cycle charts and high-speed interstate trips to the clinic during my planning periods. My days were marked by hormone surges and sperm counts and follicle measurements and Explanations of Benefits.

My dear friends, the benediction you receive at church is no joke. It is a weekly reminder to "stay rooted and established in love" (Ephesians 3:18) and to always acknowledge "Him who is able to do immeasurably more than all we ask or imagine" (Ephesians 3:20). Because I had a well-pressed medical professional sitting in front of me predicting my future, I placed my hope at her feet. Sure, I thanked God for bringing this option into our lives, but it was a sidebar gratefulness. No one but me could tell the difference. In my heart, I was still saving up the big "thank you" for delivery of services rendered. I still refused to live in the present because the present hurt too much, and God was in the present and He seemed to be ignoring me. We sat in opposite corners. It would take years to be thankful for the hard stuff. But years are better than never. And though practice doesn't make perfect, it does make for a gentler pace.

So, practice the stillness even if you don't feel it. Breathe deeply and sit with God even if you can't pray a word. The Claw will eat your money and offer promises it can't give. I wish I'd know that then.

Guiding Questions

1. How do you distract yourself from your needs with action?

2. Outline your agenda for your life here for the next year.
3. How could you give over each piece of this to God, Hannah-style?

Scripture

- 1 Samuel 1:1–20
- Ephesians 3:14–21

Chapter 2

"The First Step" and Miriam

This little pill was different from the others. It was not the small round yellow of birth control or the fat round white of Clomid. This little pill was blue and tiny. So tiny I always checked to make sure I'd swallowed it. My biggest fear was that I'd be flossing later and find it stuck in my teeth, an ineffectual sesame seed. It had zero side effects, except perhaps it was laced with a mild dose of cocaine. I felt energized in a way I had never experienced, jittery with hope. I cranked up the radio and rolled down my windows in November. I cooked and shopped and graded and walked with more bounce because life felt recognizable again. I had faith in "the plan." I nestled myself deeply in the soft, hand-knit protection of the future as patterned by my doctor. This is what research and foresight get you, I was sure: a Monopoly pass to motherhood.

Does anyone ever stop to think of Miriam, Moses' sister? You'd remember her if you saw the film *The Ten Commandments* with Charlton Heston. She's the one who hides in the reeds after pudgy baby Moses is placed in the basket by his mother. She's older, seven years older than her baby brother, and street-smart. She's the sister who would tell you to skip the skinny jeans in middle school and which teachers to tune out, Charlie Brown style. She'd help you survive.

Miriam's tale is not a tale of infertility; if anything, the Jewish community at this time had the polar opposite problem: They "were fruitful and multiplied greatly and became exceedingly numerous and the land was filled with them" (Exodus 1:7). "What's the problem?" you say from your mother's heart. "The more the merrier."

But it wasn't their land and the king wasn't too keen on filling up space with the help. Excess, it seems, is just as much a problem as dearth. Hence the horrific command that makes any mother or want-to-be mother seize up with the rigor mortis of righteous anger: "If you see that the baby is a boy, kill him" (Exodus 1:16). No fertility clinics for the Israelites. And no plan either. Merely survival. This is the world into which Moses was born and Miriam was witness.

To save his life, Moses' mom placed him in a basket and set him in the reeds in the shallow end of the Nile. But Miriam could not walk away from her bobbing baby brother. She wasn't that kind of girl. So she hid in the reeds to watch over him. He was only three months old. There would be no sink or swim for him. Sometimes I wonder if Pharaoh's daughter actually spotted Moses drifting in the stream or if maybe it took a nudge from Miriam. Hey, do you hear that? Is that a baby crying? Let's go take a look. And, of course, it was Miriam who politely asked, "Shall I go and get one of the Hebrew women to nurse the baby for you?" (Exodus 2:7) as she was already five steps on her way to get Moses' mommy. There, there, baby Moses, stop your crying. Kids have been lost in the supermarket longer than this. Miriam worked the whole show, the woman behind the curtain of reeds. You have to respect that kind of gumption.

This is the Miriam I carried with me through the heavy doors while the etched face of the sleeping baby looked down on me. Into the examination room I went after one charming month on the tiny pill to discover whether it had done its job in my uterus or was, in fact, just a sesame seed. There's a wand that I am not going to describe too closely here because we will have our fair share of juicy details later, except to tell you that it looks like the missing part of every male manikin, twice as long. And it is nothing to be trifled with. The ultrasound technician wields this wand to get in for a close-up to see if your follicles are ripe with eggs and ready to meet your husband's (hopefully) enthusiastic, fast, and plentiful sperm. The wand is not fun, but it is necessary. This is what I told myself while holding up the edge of my paper gown and humming a little ditty in my head so as not to sensory-process the entire intrusion. It was all for the greater good. It was going to show me the future.

Except that it didn't. There were no follicles for me. No eggs in my basket. How to adequately describe this kind of disappointment? *Crushing* isn't really it. Honestly, for me, it was a boatload of self-pity washed in on a tidal wave of guilt. Guilt that somehow I had messed it all up again. *Typical. You always slip up at the sticking point, don't you?* I said to myself while the screen flickered blankly. And then the guilt shifted to anger that I had let myself feel free and optimistic. If the hope had not been so high, the hurt would not dig so deep. *Thanks a lot, God, Jesus, you too, Holy Spirit. Way to pop my balloons.* I was the old man in *Up!*, in a house adrift, quickly losing altitude. In that moment, as I lay on the crinkly examination table, with insides throbbing, He was the Old Testament vengeful, wrathful, merciless God. Capital O and T. I let myself get duped again, but He was the duper. My trickster God. I paradoxically believed that I had enough control to have ruined our chances and also that He had masterminded my downfall.

I left the clinic that day under a cold and cloudy sky with trees more barren in each passing breeze. With three classes left to teach and a phone call to Jody to make, nothing felt doable. But I taught thesis statements and discussed universal life lessons without trying to sound trite. Later, when I finally called Jody, he took up the mantle of soother. He was not entirely surprised. He had suspected it might take more than this. I, somehow, had not. I continued on. Days and weeks passed and my time of the month came again. Very much expected.

Over the next several months when each ultrasound revealed a wasteland of inactivity, the hope dwindled and the endorphin high of the tiny blue pill petered out, leaving me with nothing but the stark reality of my nonsuccess.

This is the point in the story where Miriam would have hatched her plan. She faced her own "mission impossible" and found a creative solution. Baby boys are in danger? What safer place than the palace to stick a stowaway? Because of her, we have Moses, the one who led the Israelites out of bondage. She got that egg to stick. And then she sang and danced with the mist in her face while the sea swallowed the Egyptians in its greedy maw. She "took a timbrel in her hand, and all the women followed her, with timbrels and dancing" (Exodus 15:20), a biblical conga line.

But I was not Miriam, and by this point my bitterness had fermented into a nice liqueur, a snifter of ire. There wasn't even a sham attempt to be thankful and release it all to the wind and the will of God as Hannah had done. I did not listen to the benediction at church. No, I would not go out and do good and remember all the good that had been done to me. *You can't make me.*

Somehow, I managed to forget that God had given me Jody and a job I loved and pretty good hair and a dog who thought I was the bee's knees. Nothing had actually changed over the last few years except that I had pointed my finger at a shiny new desire and named it "mine," and when it was not placed in my hand at the proper time, I pitched a slow-burn war on thankfulness.

But here's the thing: It hurt so much. It hurt so very much. Every morning I woke up already tired by the vision of what the day would become. I was wearing down fast. What I see now is that He was prying my hand off the controls as gently as He could. He didn't want me to become one of those irritating people. You know the ones who think they've got life figured out and their way is best? They have zero empathy because how could they when struggle and weakness and wrongness are unfamiliar? They already know what car you need to buy before you pull into the lot. I am reminded of a Dr. Seuss book, *The Butter Battle Book*. In it, the Zooks and the Yooks get into a full-scale war over what side to butter their bread, basically politics and faith in a nutshell. They obliterate each other, or at least that is what we are to assume when left with an ominous blank page while the Right-Side-Up Song Girls sing: "Oh, be faithful! Believe in thy butter!" Cheery stuff. God was holding me back from the precipice of single-mindedness. It was nauseating and a little like vertigo. Bread buttering and mothering are serious stuff.

Miriam and I had more in common than I was willing to see. Yes, she got it right with baby Moses in the beginning, and she got it right with the celebration leaving Egypt. She even earned the commendation of prophetess. Not too shabby. But there's the rub. She let the plan and the "rightness" of everything go to her head. She forgot God was the one who launched Moses and led the people. She forgot she was a creature, not the creator. So later, when Moses marries a Cushite named Zipporah, she flips out. This was not part of her plan. She confers with Aaron, because that's what siblings do. They team up, and if necessary, plot against each other. Moses had fallen off the path, and Miriam was going to get him back on track. Sometimes God can scootch us safely into His hands, and sometimes He has to grab us and swing us around like King Kong. He booms from the clouds, "Why then were you not afraid to speak against my servant Moses?" (Numbers 12:8) when she disses her brother and then, to put a period on it, He gives her leprosy. Her skin became "white as snow" (Numbers 12:10). In a flash, Miriam becomes one of the untouchables . . . for a week. And then God heals her. Seven days to get her story straight. Seven days—a season to remember weakness and humility.

I do not understand how some people can learn this lesson with a case of the sniffles while others, me, must contract full-blown, limb-dropping "leprosy." But if I have learned nothing else from this rickety road, it is that comparison pitches you in the ditch. You can't stay in your lane with your eyes on the driver in the shinier car. It is not my place to know another's heart. By now I know my lessons and my needs. My particular potholes to begin paving.

I think it is our human nature to want to run with the controls until we trip and jab ourselves with the sharp end of our delusion. I'm endlessly stitching up my conceits. I need constant reminding that I am not in charge. It's an easy thing to forget. God isn't standing before us with the cue cards. He's offstage for the moment, and all He asks is that we turn and acknowledge the writer and director of the play we're in. Part of the Serenity Prayer reads, "God, grant me the serenity to accept the things I cannot change." To me, the phonetic similarities of *serenity* and *sanity* are not chance. Sanity comes when you can see what is in your control and what isn't.

It took me quite a few years to learn to feel relief when things were out of my hands. And let me tell you, I still like a plan and I still have my meltdowns when it veers off course, when I can't manage to keep my eyes open in that otherwise perfect photograph. I want to know, and decide, just a little, how the world should work. When a friend calls to tell me a former student has been diagnosed with cancer, I catch myself wondering, *Why, if it cannot be my plan, can't it at least be a gentler one?* And here's what I'm left with: The screen didn't show those happy follicles. Miriam and Moses didn't get to enter the Promised Land. But my student did get healed from the cancer, and occasionally I do keep my eyes open in that snapshot. Ultimately, it isn't for me to name the good and the bad and the why. I will jangle my timbrel a bit in relief over that one.

When you get that white-knuckled feeling, the one that makes you want to "get a grip" on life, my prayer for you is that you remember Miriam and all the times in your life that worked out despite yourself and your plan. The best gifts are the ones you don't pick out yourself. The best memories are the ones you don't manufacture. The same goes for life and all its turnings.

Guiding Questions

1. Have you ever felt guilty for something that was not in your control?
2. When have you tried to take control, as Miriam did, of your life or of another's?
3. How can you practice loosening the reins? What would it feel like to be dependent?
4. How can you practice ending the comparison game?

Scripture

- Exodus 1:6–10, 2:1–10, 15:19–21
- Numbers 12:1–16

Chapter 3

"The Happiness Equation" and the Bleeding Woman

When all the pills you pop fizzle out, what do you do next? According to our RE, you move on to the hard stuff. Shots. And I don't mean the ones you take at a bar, although goodness knows those have aided in their fair share of successful conceptions. My shots were much less fun and came with possibly worse side effects. I'd take a hangover over uterine torsion any day. And they were much more expensive. Babies and money will operate like tiny dictators over your spiritual state if you let them. They are little Napoleons marching across the wide expanse of your mind, planting flags and trying to be boss. But for now, we were willing to foot the bill and I was willing to suffer the pain if it brought us closer to our goal. They say the easy way out of a problem is to throw money at it. I don't know what problem "they" had in mind, but there was nothing easy about it.

We knew injections were the next step and were ready when the nice lady in the white coat behind the very tidy desk suggested we move on to Part B, or C, or D, or whatever step we were now on in the master plan. We had slipped a few rungs down the ladder in confidence and needed a move forward. We weren't looking for checkmate, just a pawn in the right direction. The shots were a surefire way to get those stubborn follicles to unclench. Apparently even my innards have separation anxiety. But we just needed them to let go of a few eggs. I wasn't asking for a baker's dozen, just one or two and call it a day.

I sat there in her office that was always too cold, and clutched my purse because Jody had his hands in his pockets. Despite the fact that I had braced myself for this, I felt rigid, with a chilly anger. Why do I have to torpedo my body in order to get it to cooperate? Why couldn't it just do me this small favor? Why must everything be uphill, both ways, in the snow? But by the time Jody did grab my hand as we stood to leave, I had rallied enough to accept this as our new tunnel to dig. We were given several prescriptions and a phone number on the way out. In case you are wondering, you couldn't just swing by your local Walgreens and pick up these drugs. These were high-octane. If a semi were hauling them, it would have all the little labels on the side: FLAMMABLE, HAZARDOUS CHEMICALS, KEEP UPRIGHT, DO NOT STORE UNDER PRESSURE. These little rocket launchers would be shipped directly to our house.

It was a mercilessly cold afternoon when I pulled into our gravel drive after work to find a lonely box sitting in the middle of our carport. It was the opposite of nondescript. Bedecked with FRAGILE, HANDLE WITH CARE, THIS SIDE UP, and REFRIGERATE IMMEDIATELY stickers, it held court for the world to see. It was so heavily labeled, I crept up to it like someone from the bomb squad. After dragging it into our kitchen as gently as a box can be dragged across concrete and up three steps, I took the scissors to its soft underbelly. Styro-foam peanuts oozed out like the guts of a fish. Half an hour later the kitchen floor was covered in 15 syringes that came in 2 different gauges, a red 5-quart disposable needle trash can, 4 glass vials of medication, and a vacuum-sealed syringe that had to be refrigerated "immediately." And for good measure, they included cotton balls, alcohol swabs, and many, many instruction sheets. At this point I looked at the dog and had to genuinely ask, "*Is* there such a thing as a prescription cotton ball?"

Later that night after cracking the instruction code with Jody's help, I stared again at my paraphernalia, the not-so-tiny needle-minions sent to do my RE's bidding. It took up an entire counter's length in the kitchen and the butter drawer in the fridge. And this was one month's supply. On a side note, the syringes and everything else eventually moved to our bed-room for obvious reasons. You don't cook in a pharmacy and you don't shoot up in the kitchen, ideally.

So the routine began. With the first pink light of sunrise, I would pull milk and a glass vial of medicine from the refrig-erator door. The milk was for my coffee, the medicine for the squishiest, most sensitive part of my belly. Remember those fitness tests you had to take in gym where they whipped out plastic forceps to measure the fat on your arm and stomach? Do they still do that? I sincerely hope not. We don't need that kind of pressure, literally or figuratively. That's the inch of skin, still warm from the shower, that I took a good grip on, just to the right or the left of the belly button, gave a good alcohol rubdown, and jabbed at with the needle like a lady at her needlepoint. It was quick and awkward, but truthfully, I barely felt it. Over the weeks, I began looking forward to that sting. Pain was gain, right?

Jody was notably absent for this part of the process. Not because he was squeamish. He always offered to do it for me, but in my head I heard the finger-wagging whisper, "You got yourself into this, now get yourself out." My inner self is a mean old lady brandishing a cane. Jody would be called to action later. But for now, this became my morning routine. Shower. Coffee. Shot. Some people just do yoga.

There was a woman whose story shows up in Matthew, Mark, and Luke. Despite the fact that she is not named, she must have made quite an impression. Jesus was pretty popular and controversial at this time and had been sailing around in a boat with disciples and groupies trailing behind. He had just cast all the demons out of a cliff-dwelling man, and into some pigs, who took a running leap into the water and drowned. Good for the man. Unfortunate for the pigs and the men who owned them. Naturally, Jesus was politely but firmly asked to vacate the area. So, He hopped back in His boat and drifted to the other side of the lake. I have no idea how big this lake was, but there were always people waiting on the other side, shouting "Jesus-ho" as He appeared on the horizon.

A synagogue ruler named Jairus was among the throng when Jesus docked. He was not there to criticize or provoke like many of his compatriots. He was there for his child. His daughter was dying, and death made him desperate. Only parents can know the excruciating ineffectualness of watching a sick child and being unable to help. No Band-Aid or amoxicillin would fix this. He needed someone to make a miracle happen. Because Jairus had the VIP pass as a public figure, he got to Him first. I imagine Jesus still shaking off His sea legs when He was approached with this plea: "My little daughter is dying. Please come and put your hands on her so that she will be healed and live" (Mark 5:23). Jesus agreed.

Enter our unnamed woman. She was desperate too. She had been bleeding for twelve years. A decade and some change. The source of bleeding was unclear, but the assumption is some sort of female problem. Can you imagine being on your period for twelve years? Can you imagine being on your period for twelve years in ancient Israel? Women were banished from society during their "time of the month." Miriam had been sent away for a week for being unclean because of her leprosy. This would have been 624 weeks of leprosy, and some change. The woman had been to the experts and "had suffered a great deal under the care of doctors and had spent all she had, yet instead of getting better, she grew worse" (Mark 5:26).

So she saw her chance and took it. While Jesus was following Jairus to his house surrounded by throngs of adoring or scorning citizens, she intercepted. She didn't really try to get His attention. Forget face-to-face, she just wanted to touch His cloak, like fan fanatics who want one touch of a jersey as the quarterback rushes the field. This will be me if I ever see Anne Lamott or Meryl Streep. While seemingly small, this was all it took for our desperate woman to bring her twelve years to an end: "Immediately her bleeding stopped and she felt in her body that she was freed from her suffering" (Mark 5:29). Stop for a moment. Health, after years of misery. Wholeness, after years of losing bits of yourself. Imagine that kind of relief, so much more palpable for its immediacy.

Because of the crowd pushing and jostling, no one knew

what happened at this point except the woman . . . and Jesus. Did she think she could slip one by Him? I like to think she had so much faith in His omnipotence that she knew she didn't need His full attention. His supernatural aura would do the work. But Jesus felt a connection. He felt her hurt and then her healing. So He called her out. He asked the crowd, "Who touched my clothes?" (Mark 5:30). You can picture it. Everybody looking over their shoulder as a hush fell. *What, who me?* So she fessed up and Jesus claimed the miracle. He blessed her and told her to "go in peace and be freed from your suffering" (Mark 5:34). And full of both fear and joy, she went, rejoicing all the way.

Right around the time Jody and I had launched ourselves physically, mentally, emotionally, and financially into pursuing fertility through the clinic, Jody's sister announced she was pregnant. She and I are around the same age and had begun trying around the same time. It was a comfort to know that we were on the same course and wouldn't it be awesome to have little cousins to wear matching pajamas at the grandparents' house at Christmas and wreak happy havoc at birthdays? How could any woman not go there? Who doesn't secretly want her fair share of that chaos? We were on this road together. And while her path was not exactly smooth either, here she was, very pregnant.

We had not fully told our families the details of our personal struggles. How do you talk about ovulation with your father-in-law or sperm motility with your mother, for that matter? That's not my kind of coffee talk. So my sister-in-law did not know the full extent of what we were going through, and I did not want to be the sad clown at the party. I wanted her to know I was happy for her . . . or that I was at least try-ing to be. I wished her well and was happy to envision a nice future with a niece or nephew, but I also wanted to supply a little person at the Rockwellian table. And so far, it was to no avail. I was feeling that illogicality of happiness and hurt. Good for you! Will there be enough left for me? But babies are not pie. No one can take the last slice.

So what about Jairus, the synagogue leader whose daugh-ter was on her death bed? He saw Jesus first, right? He asked politely. He needed it just as badly. Our bleeding lady was someone I would have liked to know. That kind of unwaver-ing faith, whether brought on by desperation or bravado, is pretty admirable. But Jairus' daughter died while Jesus was healing the woman. His friends told her to leave Jesus alone. Don't bother Him anymore. After all, what was the point? Did a bleeding lady trump a dying daughter?

Is it that she was just more persistent? I wondered as I thought about my sister-in-law buying maternity clothes while I poked myself with needles. Is that my takeaway lesson? Did I just not want it badly enough and God could tell? Notice here, I had and still have an uncanny ability to make someone else's news somehow about me. I'm the kid who grabs the camera and points it at her own face. Hurt can often do this. It can go two ways: It can round out your edges so you have more empathy for others, or it can harden something in you as a protection from more pain. This is the hardest lesson to learn in life, on the road to or in the middle of motherhood. How do you let yourself feel your hurt and process it so that you can continue to feel both sadness and joy in others? Empathy is dangerous. But empathy is necessary.

But because Jesus already knew our tendencies, He saw exactly where Jairus' mind went as he heard the news of his daughter's death. He knew the man needed to see the power too. And so He said, "Don't be afraid; just believe" (Mark 5:36). And He brought that daughter back from the dead.

He can do both, you know. He can heal the bleeding woman and bring back the dead daughter and let motherhood pan out for other people without subtracting from your needs. It's not an equation that has to even out. Your grace is not on a sliding scale. All the good comes from Him, and He's the only one who can do the math.

Guiding Questions

1. When have you felt like Jairus, the one whose needs are forgotten?
2. How has God let you know that He remembers you?
3. What is one way today that you can celebrate someone else even in the midst of your need?

Scripture

- Mark 5

Chapter 4

"The Success" and Elizabeth

Injecting fertility hormones into your body is not quite like Dr. Jekyll becoming Hyde, but it's close. The shots brought on waves of debilitating hot flashes that had me flapping file folders under my arms in between classes, and sometimes during if no one was looking. I cried during episodes of *Lost*, because why couldn't they understand that Sawyer was really the hero? I stood in front of the freezer with the door wide open, letting the frost cocoon me and my Häagen-Dazs bar. Suddenly, my body was a menopausal town car being driven around by the mood swings of an adolescent girl. I threw myself into teaching because it made me stop counting the days of my cycle in favor of days until the end of the grading period. Simply walking through the empty halls at 7 a.m., while the sun sent splintery rays down the corridor, centered me in a way the rest of my life did not.

One wall of my classroom was made up entirely of windows. These windows overlooked the baseball field and the football stadium and the rolling hills of Tennessee beyond. The view registered the passage of time in gentle fashion. The lush green and heat waves of late summer mellowed into orange and persimmon and the fog of autumn, which receded like a hairline to reveal the balding landscape of winter. Finally, joy of all, white blossoms and clear light would come bounding back in spring. This window view was my best thinking spot. I would lean against the bookcase, coffee in hand, and mentally gear up for the day. The hills took all my woes, absorbing them into their cushioned deep. And then the bell would ring and the show would commence. I still miss those windows. I know another teacher balances a cup of coffee on their frame now. I am jealous of her, like a cast-off lover. She stole my view.

You cannot really afford to be in the middle of a personal crisis, long or short term, as a teacher of teenagers. In the short term, it's too hard to find a substitute who will make them learn despite their best intentions not to. In the long term, too much of your own emotions will only stir the already roiling pot of teenage hormones. The good thing about high school is that it offers a temporary cure to any crisis. By its very nature, it teems with distractions. Before you can even unlock your room, a girl sits outside waiting to see what you thought about the new episode of *24*, and a boy recruits you to help perform an elaborate homecoming "ask," which takes more plotting than any marriage proposal. So, in the middle of my crisis, I had my class play a month-long game of "Survivor" while reading *Lord of the Flies*. I took my creative writing class to the botanical gardens to write and enact poetry slam sessions. We rapped in the daisies. I sponsored a tea club, where we ate scones and talked about Jane Austen and the merits of landing a man like Colin Firth. I was a whirling dervish of productivity, enjoying getting something right. This world of football games and homecoming dances and the fall plays and teacher conferences continued in their predictable pattern and I could forget the rest.

But home was another story. Jody was traveling for work. A lot. Working for an environmental management company meant any natural or manmade crisis in the near or not-so-near vicinity required his mapping skills and presence. Hurricanes, coal ash spills, hazardous chemicals dumped on the highway: Call Jody. He's your man! If he can't fix it, no one can! So more often than not, I would come home from a blessedly distracting job to an empty house. And silence. It was whiplash of the finest order. I was already feeling sorry for myself. The solitude did not help. The injections had brought on the kind of weight gain that inspired grocery baggers and church ladies to ask me if I was expecting. And I had acne. I was the woman in the drugstore shopping for anti-aging acne face wash. Such a thing does exist. And at the end of each day, I dragged my lonely, waddling, pimpled self home and talked to the dog, who was the only one there to listen.

Luckily, this hormonal roller coaster came to a stop each month. Weeks of shots would be followed by an up-close-and-personal visit with the wand when the ultrasound technician would check to see if my follicles had done their job. Had they grown to the appropriate size? Too small and there'd be no room for the egg; too big and they would turn to cysts. My womb was the Three Bears' house and my eggs, a bunch of finicky Goldilockses. This tale was getting didactic.

But lo and behold, after months of tinkering with the dosages, a miracle finally occurred. I had three follicles with eggs ripe for the picking. Let all the hormones rejoice! So one early December afternoon, I drove home at Nascar speeds to share the good news with Jody, who was, for once, home. We both stood in the middle of the kitchen, taking a minute to let it sink in that we had made it to the next step. Now came the biggest part of our chemistry experiment. I was to open that refrigerated and sealed special shot that had been nesting on my butter shelf. I was to administer it exactly twelve hours before our clinic visit the following day. Hypothetically, this shot would force those appropriately sized follicles to release those eggs so that they could be ready and waiting for Jody's swimmers the following day. I had stared greedily at the syringe for weeks. This shot didn't hurt a bit.

They say Elizabeth, who is the opening act in Luke, was already old, or as the Bible so delicately puts it, "well along in years" (Luke 1:6) by the time she got pregnant with John the Baptist. She had already been deemed barren by whoever decided such things. Somehow, I always picture a man banging a gavel, like in that episode of *The Twilight Zone* where the librarian is deemed "Obsolete." This seems especially unfair when you consider that she was probably the modern-day equivalent of, say, thirty. She and her husband, Zechariah, were good, solid religious folk. Unlike Hannah's husband, Zechariah didn't judge Elizabeth for wanting babies. Instead, being the good priest and spouse that he was, he prayed that they would be able to conceive. And one night when he was on incense duty in the temple, he got his wish. An angel appeared with congratulations, noting that his "prayer has been heard" (Luke 1:13). You are going to be a father. And you are going to have a son. And you are going to name him John. And he's "going to be filled with the Holy Spirit even from birth" (Luke 1:15). And he's going to be one of the best at preparing people for the coming of the Lord. That's a lot of information for one guy to take in. And maybe it was because of all the incense or maybe it was because he was one of those fearful people (me) who wait for the "but" in every piece of good news, whatever the case, Zechariah could not help to point out that "I am an old man and my wife is well along in years" (Luke 1:18). We all do this, don't we? We try so hard to believe in miracles, but the minute we glimpse one, we begin to rationalize it out of existence.

Gentle tip: Don't second-guess an angel. Those who can reward can also punish. The angel took Zechariah's voice, silencing him until his son would be born—the biblical version of "I don't want to hear another word out of you, young man." Thankfully, Elizabeth had her head on straight and gave credit where credit was due: "The Lord has done this for me. In these days, he has shown his favor and taken away my disgrace among the people" (Luke 1:25). And she got to be the mother of John the Baptist. And Zechariah did get to talk again, when he rasped the name "John" and blessed his new baby son. He was so deliriously happy that he even croaked out a song: "Praise be to the Lord, the God of Israel, because he has come to his people and redeemed them" (Luke 1:68).

No angel appeared to Jody when our conception time came. The process itself could not have felt less charmed. They don't leave the actual baby making up to you when they've done all the heavy work on the front end. Intrauterine insemination was the final step in this experiment, the denouement of the show. And who are we kidding? How could it feel anything but clinical when Jody had to enter a separate room at the clinic exactly half an hour before the procedure and come out with a bagged cup? There was no Marvin Gaye or gospel music humming in the background. And yet, can I tell you something? It felt spiritual and special. It felt like God was in the room with us when it all began. It was like He had laid the foundation of our jigsaw puzzle and was finally pushing in those last tricky pieces, the ones in the center that make the picture complete.

The actual procedure was beyond weird, though. Picture if you will, you and your spouse in a small, brightly lit room with tiled floors and bad art on the one wall you can see with your feet in the stirrups. At least you have learned by now to bring socks; your feet will be warm, if not dignified. Your nurse, who is in a good mood because it's Friday, reads you the stats of your husband's sperm: morphology (shape), motility (energy level: think mile time), quantity (the more the better). You want them lean, fast, and plentiful. She then checks your wristbands, because they aim to impregnate the right people with the right DNA. Once all is verified and the never-warm-enough speculum is in place, an impossibly long catheter is inserted into your uterus. At the end is a syringe containing the verified swimmers. There is no position, mood lighting, soothing image, or soft music to make this comfortable. You've just got to grin and bear it. But there was a moment, right after the nurse told me it was finished, that I felt a sense of comfort, a sense of rightness despite the wrongness of the scene. And then I waited ten minutes, got dressed, and went back to work. That right there was more surreal than the rest of it. From exam table to topic sentences in an hour flat.

Waiting is not my forte. The fourteen-day lag time between procedure and result might as well have been nine months of angel-imposed silence. I was a world unto myself, every day free to execute a self-analysis and study the results. I would think I felt a twinge and pray it was the baby settling in, or I'd notice a weird smell at the Chinese restaurant and swear it was the pregnancy hormones kicking in. What Chinese restaurant doesn't have a weird smell? But that was neither here nor there. I soldiered on, lamenting the fact that I felt more pregnant on Day 1 than Day 10. Then again, Day 12 was chock-full of hormones. I could have eaten my arm and sweated out children if you'd asked me to. There is no exit to the maze that is the mind of the possibly artificially inseminated woman. But the two weeks did pass and I went in for the blood test. I even paid the extra fee to have the results rushed because I was not going to wait another second for the truth to be revealed. I was Zechariah bursting at the seams.

The thing about IUIs is that you can't do them one right after the other. I had, after all, been injecting myself with highly potent hormones. My body wasn't going to bounce back from that like the arcade game with the gophers that you whack with a mallet. My gophers had migraines and went into hiding every other month. Which was why I wanted so desperately for this to work. Stopping and waiting would feel like starting all over again. Not a move forward, but another grueling ride on the stationary bike. So when the nurse called to tell me the results were negative, she was so sorry, call my RE during business hours tomorrow to schedule a follow-up appointment, I felt sucker-punched. I sat with the numbness until it ramped up into a weeping rage, which at some point drained away, leaving me a hiccupping mess on the kitchen floor. Which was where Jody found me that evening, kicking at the syringe container and all cried out. And still, still, after all this I managed to call the office and make an appointment. The appointment would, of course, reveal many cysts, the only thing my body grew well, which led my doctor to tell me what I already knew: I would have to take a month off to "let everything quiet down." Clearly, she couldn't hear the screaming in my head.

So I taught and laughed at my students' jokes and read *Brave New World* alone on the couch when Jody was out of town, and I reminded myself to breathe in and out. I even prayed a little, mostly angry whispers in the car to and from work. And I did this for five months: the shots, the exams, the IUIs, and the waiting game until one day just short of Easter when everything was new life and resurrection and baby chicks and pastel bunnies, I got the call: The third time was the charm. IUI number three would become our April blessing. It turned out that repeating the same thing over and over was not insanity, but actually protocol. I do not know what made that time different. Perhaps one of Jody's sperm had a good night's rest. Perhaps my uterus was extra squishy from all the ice cream and egg salad I'd been eating. It didn't matter in the end, because I was finally pregnant. The silence was over. I was singing with Zechariah and rejoicing like Elizabeth.

When Elizabeth was pregnant with John, her cousin Mary, who was also pregnant, paid a visit. As Mary approached, John did this great gymnastic floor routine in Elizabeth's womb, which caused her to exclaim, "Blessed are you among women, and blessed is the child you bear!" (Luke 1:42). John's excitement was infectious. Can't you just picture it? One woman sidling up to her cousin, who is currently harboring a little peach-sized Jesus. Maybe she placed her hand on her own stomach when John gave a particularly well-aimed high five. Elizabeth could not help but revel in it, saying, "Blessed is she who has believed that what the Lord has said to her will be accomplished!" (Luke 1:45). She's overcome with thanksgiving. This is how I felt, my friends, when we heard the news. Suddenly, I was brimming with awe and gratefulness and a sudden kindred spirit with all the other pregnant women in the world. It was no longer a club to which I was denied membership. We were all on this bizarre journey together.

Because I was no longer an "infertile," I was happy to celebrate with my sister-in-law as she shared truly gruesome anecdotes of the morning sickness that was to come: stories of partially digested burritos reconstituted in the bathroom of a Mexican restaurant and days without much but water and . . . water. Notwithstanding the fact that both our families already knew each step in our trajectory, I still sent every one of them a somewhat confusing pregnancy announcement: one extra-large plastic Easter egg housing a Christmas ornament marked with my December due date. They laughed and took my ornament/egg in good stride. I spent a lot of time that April sitting in the grass with my back against the baseball fence, letting the sun warm my face and quietly giving thanks. Despite, or maybe because of, my former angst, I recognized this for what it was, a gift from God. I was Zechariah, undeserving but still rejoicing with Elizabeth at the other end of the rainbow. And despite what came later, I do not regret any of it.

You will have your moments of skepticism and your

moments of gratefulness on this road, my friend. You will be both Zechariah and Elizabeth. God recognizes all your sides, the multifaceted you that He created, and He loves you. *He loves you.* It's important to let that part sink in, because it's easy to forget when the things to be thankful for don't line up to be counted. My prayer for you is that you can practice feeling loved by God just as much as you practice all the rest.

Guiding Questions

1. How have you rationalized miracles in your own life?
2. When have you felt God calling you to silence and stillness rather than action?
3. How might you practice thankfulness and patience when your prayer remains unanswered?

Scripture

- Luke 1:5–25, 1:39–45, 1:68

The Waiting

Chapter 5

"The Loss" and Naomi

Naomi had her fair share of difficulties. It might not have been quite on par with the slave state of Egypt or forty years in the desert, but living in Bethlehem during a famine was not paradise. Forget ordering groceries online or take-out curry, this was fighting over the last drops of oil and flour. So she and her husband and two grown sons packed up the proverbial U-Haul and headed out of Judah. They landed in Moab, which was not exactly Israelite-friendly. The king had, in fact, called in Balaam, the soothsayer, to curse God's people. I think he would have set up Mounties with guns at the border checkpoints if he could have. The Balaam mission didn't go as planned. After verbal and physical abuse, the donkey he was riding quit the mission and literally told him to chill out. Looking down her long snout with sad eyes like Eeyore, she said, "What have I done to make you beat me these three times?" (Numbers 22:28). That'll get your attention. It got Balaam's, who finally noticed the angel in the road. Why do we never notice the angel until we're bearing down on it at eighty miles an hour? The angel informed Balaam that Eeyore actually saved his life: "If she had not turned away, I certainly would have killed you by now, but I would have spared her"

(Numbers 22:33). Good ole donkey. With his body and mind readjusted for travel, Balaam headed home, with hands in the air praising the God of the Hebrews. So much for the plans of kings and men.

This was the atmosphere that Naomi and her family entered—a land full of natives suspicious and resentful of their intrusion. But they made it work, because they were hungry and because women like Naomi don't just sit down and cry. I picture Dorothea Lange's black-and-white photograph of the migrant mother, living in the dust bowl, full of grit and gristle and scrapping her way through life. And it works. Imagine how Naomi must have felt navigating this new land. She had to learn all over again the closest well, the best vendor for oil, the people who would sell to a foreigner and the people who pretended not to see her as she walked by. It must have been lonely. She must have been scared, especially after her husband died once they arrive. Some people crumble under pressure and some harden, like diamonds or coal. Naomi was the latter and still managed to marry off both her sons to nice Moabite girls. Ruth and Orpah seemed immune to their people's prejudice. And thus followed a decade of prosperity for the little family.

Hard work coupled with resourcefulness can get you that kind of life. Or at least that's what I was raised to believe. If you want to be number one and get accepted into a top-ranked college, you can't hit cruise control. I was full throttle from birth to, well . . . I still am for the most part, unless Jody steps in and forces me to slow down to an acceptable speed. Black-and-white, all-or-nothing, perfection-or-destruction, this is me.

The Waiting

So when we found out we were pregnant, it was like being handed a fast-forward button. I have just enough manic-depressiveness about me that I can get mired in all the gunky badness. But if one thing goes right, tiny or huge, I'm the Sunshine Care Bear, the Christmas elf singing loud for all to hear. So I fast-forwarded past the part of the conversation with the nurse that said my numbers were still a little low and to proceed with caution. Like a young, naïve Superman, I felt immune to dark proclivities.

Joy is tricky business. If you put it in the right place, with God, and let it unfold naturally, it can be a beautiful gift. If you put it on a thing, an event, or a person and suction yourself to it like cling wrap, you're in for a world of trouble.

I went into the clinic for a second blood test two days after the first to see if my numbers had risen appropriately and to check my hormone levels, which had been on the low side. Yes, I will pay the extra fee again because, no, I do not want to wait an extra day to receive my results. The phone buzzed later during seventh period. I was breaking every rule in the good teacher handbook by keeping my cell phone mortared to my side while issuing demerits to students playing Candy Crush under the table—but I couldn't help it. Babies over video games, right?

During the last period of the day on a Friday afternoon, I stepped out and took the call. Numbers looked great! Joy validated. The relief was so sudden, I felt light-headed. I could now wait four days to come back in for another blood test, and if that looked good, they would schedule an ultrasound in two weeks to check on our little nugget and try to catch a flickering heartbeat. Things were moving along.

As you already know, we did not wait the requisite twelve weeks before we told our family the good news. In fact, after a trip to Target with my phone set to Pinterest, I parceled together my "good news eggs" and handed them out to the immediate family the following day when we gathered to watch my nephew play baseball. I was truck, truck, truckin' along and setting my own timeline now. The sky was filled with clouds so perfect, they looked fake, those soothingly onomatopoeic cumulus clouds. The grass where we spread our coats was Kermit green. My mom was the only one to open her egg and figure it out at once. Moms usually do. Cue the "happy tears." It was in these years of infertility that I first began to view my mother as a person apart from her role as mom. It was comforting to see that this was not all she was, to see that this was not all that I needed to be, to be complete. She was a person who played Bunco and yelled in traffic and read Tom Clancy and hated Tom Cruise and loved cream sauces. She was herself, and on this day, she was all those things wrapped in a tissue package of grandmotherly happiness. The day was perfect. My nephew won the game. We went out for burgers.

And then the next day, I started bleeding. There's no good way to describe the feeling that something is wrong; it grips you wordlessly. When I woke up, I knew the wetness between my legs was not a weak bladder. I knew and did not want to look. Instead, I lay in bed and prayed that it would be anything but what I suspected it was. I put up everything I had for God to use as leverage. I would never complain again about Jody or lazy students or traffic or cooking. Please, God, just let it be my imagination. And then I moved on from God to Google, where I checked for every possible way that bleeding this early could be okay. And then I got up and went to the bathroom to verify what I already knew.

This would be the first of many calls to the on-call doctor. No, there was nothing they could do for me. Do not come in. It was a standard response though spoken kindly. Even if they did an ultrasound, there would be nothing to see yet. I couldn't help but wonder, after we hung up and stared at our hands for a while, how something that had sent our world into Technicolor could still be too small to see? After hours of the bad kind of Googling about first-term pregnancy complications, none of which I wanted to remember, I shut my laptop and my eyes and asked Jody to hold my hand and pray for this baby because I just couldn't do it. My prayers and gambles hadn't worked in all the years I'd had cards to play, or so it felt. There were both too many words and not enough, and I had lost the voice to name them. So, we sat on our couch under the picture window in the front room and he prayed for our moth-wing hope while I shrouded myself in a blanket, wrapping up all the pieces of me.

By the next day, the bleeding was down to mild spotting and the numbers showed another jump, not quite a doubling, but good enough for them, and good enough for this girl, who was back to Care Bear status. It is exhausting to live this way and I do not recommend it. Letting your emotions fling you around like a yo-yo is nauseating, a dizzying slide show instead of a life. But I was full of hormones and desperate for hope so I let the good news carry me away. By this time, Jody's family had received the egg announcements in the mail and were calling all day to congratulate us. I glossed over the weekend's traumatic events, more than willing to put them behind us. Jody, true to form, was more matter-of-fact about our situation. I gave him the stink eye. Because I'm that kind of Care Bear too.

That afternoon, I stopped by a maternity store because it was on my way home from work, sort of. I didn't buy anything. But they did have bumps in various sizes for you to strap on at your leisure. I spent a long time admiring my three- and six- and nine-month self in the floor-length mirror. I never told Jody this part. He'd had enough crazy.

This was, I decided, going to be my time of celebration after all the hard work. I was Naomi and this was my golden decade. I continued to spot off and on, but as the doctors kept saying, there was nothing to do but wait for the ultrasound, and I wasn't worried. I certainly felt pregnant. Nausea. Increased sensitivity to smells. Clothes tighter. Dizziness. If you are already doing the math, then you know that I was the equivalent of about a month pregnant. If it was up to my powers of imagination, I could magic a baby right into existence. I told the news to my closest coworkers, those fellow English teachers who spoke the love language of Keats and Kesey and Kerouac. They had covered for me through doctors' appointments and traffic jams and unexplained weeping sessions. They deserved to be in the know. This baby was a team effort.

Naomi got a decade, and I got two weeks. I went by myself to the ultrasound. Jody would have gone, but was out of town. He planned to make the following visit at the eight-week mark, which would be with a regular OB-GYN. We were more than ready to graduate to the normal world of pregnancy protocol. There was no wand this time and I prepared myself on the exam table for the regular old warm goo on the belly. We were moving on up. This particular technician knew me by now. We often made small talk while I tried not to feel awkward. She had kids that went to my brother's old high school. She was nice.

They always get real quiet once the ultrasound begins. It's dark in there, like the movie theater right before the film begins and only the runner lights are lit. I remembered to breathe and stared at the ocean on the screen, waiting for my eyes to adjust to its depths. She pointed to the sac and then the murky yolk nestled in the center. And then she paused, "hmmm"-ed, and then checked the chart in front of her. She asked how far along I was. "Six weeks," I said in a faraway voice. I was not looking at her, still mesmerized by the tiny bubble on the screen.

"Hmmms" are never good in the medical profession. She noted, almost offhandedly, that we should be seeing a heartbeat by now and she would show my results to the RE. They would probably have me come back in for one more ultrasound before releasing me to the great blue yonder of the OB. And then she followed it all up with her own story of her first ultrasound when no heartbeat was detected. As the story goes, despite the early absence, after a long weekend out of town, bam, there it was, strong as an ox. "He's going to college next year, did you know?" She wiped the gel off my stomach. "Some are just slow starters," she said, and left me to get dressed and pray my story would follow hers in form if not detail.

Padded as my news was with the tech's success, I didn't feel the usual qualms that had been my default in this motherhood game. That grit kicked into high gear and I was going to pray and visualize that heartbeat into existence like the scene in *Peter Pan* where the audience has to *clap clap clap* for Tinkerbell to wake up. What must it have been like for Naomi, still grieving for her husband but knowing she had to be the matchmaker for her sons? She would have had to organize weddings, which could only have made her remember her own. We do not know what kind of marriage Naomi and Elimelech had, but given her strength of character, I can imagine she would have landed herself an equally strong catch, like two grizzlies meeting in a stream. It must have been bittersweet marrying off the boys alone. Her grab at joy worked well, though. That was my plan too.

By this point we had stopped giving the family play-by-plays. It was too much to tell and there were too many varying responses to hear. No one needs more than one finger at a time on the pulse of their own emotional state. But the night before our next ultrasound, I woke for a midnight bathroom break (they seemed to be happening more and more lately), only to find a toilet of blood. It was a deep murky red, not the pink kind as in *Jaws*. You can't clap your way through that one. It was at this point I wished our family knew the ups and downs. I wished I could call my mom and have her mend me like she used to. Please kiss the fear and make it better. It was a long time until daylight. I lay with my legs propped up, shaking and trying to use gravity to keep something in that seemed to desperately want out. There was more blood than I could have imagined.

No one tells you that loss is so messy.

I don't remember praying at this point. Shock and fear and adrenaline were pounding too loudly for thought.

The Waiting

The morning was sunny and mellow in its spring-ness. The daffodils seemed to turn their heads away from my darkness. Jody drove while I tried to lie very still across the backseat, as if that could hold things together, hold things in. But the center cannot hold. I looked at the ceiling, a tiny strip of fabric dangling near the sunroof. I wanted to peel it off. It would feel good to rip something.

This time an RE performed our ultrasound. He wasn't our usual doctor. He was, in fact, the head of the practice. They brought in the manager, to mollify the scene everybody assumed was coming. He didn't say anything as he ran the probe over my stomach. I let the darkness take me and did not watch the screen. And then it was over. He clicked off the monitor, patted my leg, and told me to meet him in the examination room across the hall. He'd like to do a physical exam, he said. Jody squeezed my hand so hard, I felt the bones rub together. It felt good.

In a new room with another piece of bad wall art, the paper blanket cracked like gunshots as I wrapped it around my legs. My hands were still shaking and the air-conditioning was on full blast, my own arctic pit. The cold had me clenched like a body already in rigor mortis. I didn't want to be examined, to open myself up so this stranger could invade a space that should have been a secret seal over a growing child. It felt like a violation. All of it did, from the very beginning, really. Too many needles and insertions and removals of too many things for a body to handle. But more than that too, many hopes had been given and many destroyed. Too many times, I had let myself feel encouraged. I wished they'd all leave me alone, Jody included, so that I could curl up, turn off the lights, and sleep for a year. But I let the doctor open my legs and perform the necessary duties to make the pronouncement official. Miscarriage.

While I folded my arms around myself, already an empty space, the doctor cited the statistics of miscarriages in the reproductive lifespan of a woman. About one in five, if you are wondering, which I wasn't. As he took off his gloves and washed his hands, he said it did not mean our chances to conceive were any less than before and was, in fact, proof that my body knew what to do and could make a baby. He patted my shoulder, leaving it smelling of disinfectant, before walking us to the door.

Did you know that *blunder* is a synonym for *miscarriage*? As if this were not really a baby, but instead a stumbling along the path. It was still just an embryo in this stage, not even a fetus yet, the doctor made sure to note. As if the manipulation of words could work out the hurt like a stubborn knot. How many mothers have lost and still love the not-yet baby?

Naomi's ten years of happiness ended with the deaths of both her sons. The seasons of her life moved through mountains and valleys, from famine in Judah to feast in Moab to famine again for her and her widowed daughters-in-law. How was a widow supposed to live without support in a land that would never treat her as anything more than a foreigner, a fringe element? There was no such thing as relying on the kindness of strangers. So Naomi did what any desperate woman would do—she went home. But Ruth and Orpah were Moabites, and she could see that they would be facing the exact same scenario as she did in Moab if they entered Bethlehem, a land alien to them. And they would not be flanked by men like Naomi had been. She knew what they were getting into, and somewhere along that "road that would take them back to the land of Judah" (Ruth 1:7), maybe minutes or miles down the path after she had tested their loyalty, Naomi turned to them and said, "Go back, each of you, to your mother's home. May the Lord show kindness to you, as you have shown your dead and to me. May the Lord grant that each of you will find rest in the home of another husband" (Ruth 1:8–9). Be gone and be at peace.

This is the equivalent of the rescued rabbit, now rehabilitated and dropped off in the woods by the side of the road. It will be better off in the wild now, the Good Samaritan thinks, but the damage is already done. The rabbit has been tamed. Naomi knew she couldn't provide for these two women, so she tried to cut them loose. But she loved them and they her, and she had no one left. When they ignored her and kept going, she "shooed" them away with reason. She argued, "Why would you come with me? Am I going to have any more sons, who would become your husbands? Return home, my daughters" (Ruth 1:1–12). Go, back into the wild with you.

But logic dissolved, as it always does when circumstances kick it to the curb. Like a tin can full of holes, it will always seep emotion. Naomi cried like a little girl, saying, "It is more bitter for me than for you, because the Lord's hand has gone out against me!" (Ruth 1:13). Preach it, sister. That's exactly how I felt. It was more bitter that I had tasted happiness with this pregnancy than if it had never happened at all. It hurt so much worse. Nothing could top this loss. When we arrived home after the "confirmation" of our miscarriage, I was still bleeding and cramping and sticky from the ultrasound gel.

I wanted nothing more than to be left alone, hollowed out. But Ruth stuck with Naomi. She had become her home and Moab, the forest. She had been tamed. Sometimes I wonder, when Orpah agreed to return to her family and Ruth vowed her undying loyalty, if Naomi was actually glad, or a little irritated. I like to relish my misery solo. I want time to walk that dusty road and think and mourn and plan the rest of my life without company. That is what hardness does. It can create a diamond, but a diamond isn't soft. It is unmalleable perfection.

Naomi clearly had not worked out her issues by the time she reached home. She told anyone she met, "Call me Mara, because the Almighty has made my life very bitter" (Ruth 1:20). If anyone had seen me in the days and weeks following the miscarriage, they would not have noticed a thing. I taught and ran and cooked and remembered to shower and grade and speak to Jody in the morning and at night. But I was an eye looking inward. It was somehow worse when the bleeding stopped, like it had all been an illusion. There was nothing left to cry over.

But Naomi, despite all the loss and the starting over, somehow once again picked herself back up enough to play "Yenta" to Ruth and Boaz. She orchestrated a marriage and became a grandmother. The women in the town, perhaps the same ones whom she told to call her Mara, exclaimed, "Praise be to the Lord, who this day has not left you without a kinsman-redeemer. May he become famous throughout Israel! He will renew your life and sustain you in your old age. For your daughter-in-law, who loves you and who is better to you than seven sons, has given him birth" (Ruth 4:14–15). This little grandson was Obed, grandfather to David, Israel's future king. The scene ends as "Naomi took the child, laid him in her lap and cared for him" (Ruth 4:16). It is hard to be bitter when holding a child.

But of course, I had no child to hold. And even in motherhood, bitterness has its season. Toddlerhood and teens perhaps.

Famine to feast to famine to feast for Naomi. It seems like too much for one woman to handle. Yet this is how the Lord moves. I have taken the long road in learning this lesson. Something in my mind so wants it to be linear—a steady and reasonable incline to heaven. Life should be like the birds and the bees' song: "First comes love, then comes marriage, then comes babies in the baby carriage." When we lost this little one, I could not see my way past it. All the good along the way dissolved, sunk in tears and pain that grew like a weed, choking out the light. My grit hadn't gotten me anywhere and neither had God's grace, or so it felt. In that moment, I only saw the void. I let the peace decay because it didn't lead uninterruptedly to joy. I could not, at the time, see the good that had been and what, perhaps, could be again.

And that's okay too. God let Naomi be bitter. And it's not like little Obed erased the loss of her husband and sons. God doesn't get offended by our moods. He is not so small, with His nose pressed to the map, that He can't see our hurts while also seeing past them. He gets it. Even Jesus asked for a reprieve from the pain and fear in Gethsemane. Stoicism is not God's way. It is why those chin-up responses to heartbreak—"It's all part of God's plan"—while true, never fully work. And that's why He will always give you the time and space to process what needs to be felt and thought and yelled.

After our miscarriage, I needed to be numb and then raw and then bitter before I could trust again. It was a long road back from this place despite the outward steps forward in my pursuit of motherhood. The depression and wary distrust of God were real. It is only now as I look back that I can identify with Naomi at the end. All I can say to you, if you are in the middle of the empty road of infertility, or the busy intersection of little kids, or the side of the rode of the teen years with your thumb out, is this: From famine to feast, my friends. Whatever the plan, in this life and thereafter, you will be cared for, you will be safe, you will be home.

Guiding Questions

1. When have you felt grief for the loss of a loved one or the loss of a dream?
2. What coping mechanisms have you used to work though disappointment? Did they work? Why or why not?
3. Naomi had Ruth and Boaz, and later, Obed. Who are your people, your tribe, whom God has brought into your life to love you for better or worse?

Scripture

- Numbers 22:21–41
- Ruth 1, 4:13–16

Chapter 6

"The Fallout" and the Woman Who Anoints Jesus with Oil

Days grew longer as the rest of the world came back to life. Winter and taxes had ended, and nature rallied itself for summer. Aspiring gardeners planted peppers and tomato plants with Home Depot tags still attached and left to flutter in the breeze. Lawnmowers roared to life and sprinklers *tsk-tsk-tsked* their endless arcs. And in the middle of exam review in early May, I snuck out yet again to meet Jody at the fertility clinic. While our RE spoke, rehashing the well-hewn history, I studied her face. It helped that she never looked me in the eye. I could observe at my leisure. That face was a wonder. She'd clearly had work done. The lines did not quite meet at proper intersections. Yet the overall effect was almost perfect. Pristine. I marveled at the marvel of modern science. It's amazing what humans have managed to do. We have circumnavigated the aging process, viral epidemics, nuclear war, and Wi-Fi. We are phenoms, a society full of prodigies, budding with potential.

That was where my mind wandered while she began her suggestions for our future. Hurt and aching with an anger I could not really name or aim at an individual, I sat and pretended to listen, knowing she would make the ultimate call and not really caring what it was. Did we continue with IUIs? After all, we had to count that last one as a success despite the outcome, she reminded us. Despite the outcome. And it was less medical intervention and much less costly than other alternatives. *Except natural conception*, I thought, and caught a look from Jody that said he was thinking the same thing.

In the end, she recommended we move on to the biggie, the one that was supposed to be the last resort that we would never need to get to, the only one that required more waivers than skydiving. In vitro fertilization. This was DEFCON 1. We balked at the number of steps, the level of drugs, the surgeries, the cost, oh, the cost. But her rationale came down to primarily one thing: safety, namely mine.

You see, I have Grade A eggs-ellent eggs, and when medicinally prompted, my follicles hatched a great bundle into the uterine ether. The problem with this scenario is that I am not, in fact, a chicken, and if you blindly shoot sperm into an atmosphere like that, there's a distinct possibility I'd be the next sextuplet mom on reality television. It's like popcorn, really. Throw the bag in the microwave and you can't control how many kernels pop. Better to cook it on the stove, slowly and closely monitored, so you can add as much or as little as you need, give or take a few. I didn't want to be the popcorn bag. Suddenly and voraciously, I wanted some control back. I needed to know we were doing everything humanly and scientifically possible to keep myself and this hypothetical baby safe. So we took our pamphlets and waivers and price sheets and contracts home and told her we'd think about it.

But at this point, who are we kidding? There wasn't really anything to think about. We were on a trajectory at a speed that felt impossible to slow down, because slowing down might as well be stopping the ride altogether. Jody prayed about it. I tried. Do you remember that eighties movie *Drop Dead Fred* with the girl from *Fast Times at Ridgemont High*? Fred was her imaginary friend from childhood who reappears years later and flips her life upside down. God was my imaginary friend and I was screaming, "Stop following me around already. I can *handle* it." It all seemed unfathomable, both the next step and what had already come before, but I still didn't want help. In the end, we signed the forms and took our relationship with our bank to the next level. We committed to IVF.

After Jesus had outed Himself as the son of God and was nearing the end of His three years of miracles and inspirational talks and after He had picked and trained the disciples, He came to a town called Bethany. A woman approached Him while He was at the table eating in the house of Simon the Leper and poured an entire jar of perfume on His head. The anointing with oil was common back then, much like the washing of feet. It was hot and dirty and you ate reclining next to the table. Whatever smells you cultivated or picked up along the way came to the table with you. There was no Febreeze for your Chacos. So you dabbed on some scented oil and rinsed off your toes before sticking them in your fellow diner's face. But what this woman did was different. This was "expensive perfume" (Matthew 26:6), and it was the whole jar. That was a lot of scent and a lot of money all in one go. The disciples immediately got their feathers ruffled. Like little old ladies shaking their heads at wasted leftovers, they pursed their lips and whispered among themselves: "Why this waste? This perfume could have been sold at a high price and the money given to the poor" (Matthew 26:8–9). Jesus was so patient. I bet He didn't even sigh at the thought of how much work He still had left with these guys. They had seen the sick healed and the Pharisees shamed and the prostitutes and tax collectors welcomed. Yet they still missed the point. When this woman anointed Jesus, they saw only waste. How many people could be clothed and fed with the money that perfume could bring? How many widows could be cared for with such expense? For them, life, even charity, was still a give-and-take. I thought so too, still grieving my loss while creeping toward the future. What would I need to give, in order to take the child I longed for?

The process of telling our close family and friends of our miscarriage was brutal. Some feedback, though stark, was welcome, like the cleansing sting of alcohol on a fresh wound. Our pastor and his wife came to our home and sat on the couch where I had cried and Jody had prayed. I think back to the tableaus we must have formed through that front window over the years and feel a bit sorry for the dog walkers. Truthfully, I hadn't wanted visitors that day. It was a Sunday afternoon and all I wanted was to shut the blinds, turn on the TV, and forget everything. Is it still Plato's cave if you choose it? I was tired of being blinded by reality. But I wrapped myself in that same old blanket and let them pray for us. They prayed for healing for me and hope and finally, bravely, success in the near future. Sometime, when our eyes were shut, Jody took his hand away from mine. A sideways glance caught him wiping a tear. Just one. There was no noise, no snot, no hiccupping like I was wont to do. But it cut through something in me that had been frozen since the cold day in the examination room. It brought me out of myself for a millisecond to catch someone else's hurt. Jody's not a crier. I can count on one hand the tears he's shed. He saves them for when they matter. This was not just my fight to fight. It was a slap of realization, but a gentle one, like someone waking you from a faint. I'm not sure anything else during that time could have brought me out of my grief and up for air like that one glimpse into Jody's pain. As we talked and prayed and passed around tissues, it unhitched a bit of the burden. Unfortunately, not all the confessional moments were this healing.

You know those people who can't fight the urge to fill in the silence after bad news? Like the dead air needs spritzing with an aphorism? It's an understandable reaction. There is always the need to put an end to the ringing hollowness of gloom and doom. We got, "Well at least you weren't very far along," and "It's all part of God's plan," and "I bet you'll get pregnant right away." All these things might be true, but hearing it taped up and delivered like a regifted wedding present feels like getting schooled by your mom. You smile and nod and do not say any of the things that would make the conversation last a second longer.

We knew some of these conversations would be awkward and torturous. Miscarriage is exactly that. But we weren't prepared for the general reaction to our starting IVF. After the miscarriage, we had had a long discussion about whom we wanted to give updates and breaking news bulletins to. Who were the vital recipients? It came down to (1) a tiny number of family members, particularly those from whom we might need both prayers and money, (2) a handful of friends who had already walked this far with us, and (3) a few coworkers who would need to know for practical purposes. One of my closest coworkers joked, as we sat facing each other in student desks at lunch, that she hoped we weren't going to try for one of those "test tube babies" because that felt like "bad juju." How do you proceed? Well, now that you mention it, we are, in fact, conjuring that exact test tube juju. It was uncomfortable on both ends and ended with nervous laughter. All family members brought up the financial strain, as they had already seen us both panic about money. My mom, more than the rest, worried about the stress and anxiety it had created for me. It was probably similar to watching the teenage me push for top marks all over again, but medicated. Some comments caught me completely off guard, like a spiderweb across your face in the dark. One in particular stands out in my mind: "So if this doesn't work, what's your plan? Will you adopt?" IVF seemed like such a huge undertaking. I could not fathom thinking past it. To jump to adoption from the very get-go felt like jumping ship before leaving the dock.

Here's the thing: Every single one of these people loved us more and better than we deserved. The reason these comments felt so resoundingly off-key was that they were our own doubts as well. They were the twangy notes of our own consciousness. We knew IVF would hurt us financially and that medicine does often feel like scary and possibly dangerous magic and that stress would hit hard and that other people adopt. Yet we were still choosing this and trying not to feel like stubborn children ignoring all reason. But we had prayed about it, and despite the lack of the neon "yes" we wished would appear, we felt called to do it.

Emptying that complete jar of perfume on Jesus' head did not look like a smart move. It could have been sold and then put to use in a variety of perhaps more practical ways. The disciples had that right. But Jesus recognized her action for what it was, an extravagant display of faith. He said, "She has done a beautiful thing to me. The poor you will always have with you, but you will not always have me" (Matthew 26:10–11). She proved that she believed He would do what He came to do. He would die for the sins of all the people and so she emptied that perfume on Jesus to "prepare [him] for burial" (Matthew 26:12). This was not a moment for practicality. This was a moment for faithful extravagance.

In this season, God pointed us on the path toward IVF despite many good reasons against it. I was not in a place to pray it through like I should. There were too many conflicting emotions and too many pains still fresh, but I sat in the silences to see what God would do with my heart. And I trusted Jody, who prayed for us both. It seems odd to say that IVF was our leap of faith, when many would argue that such a level of medical intervention takes matters out of God's hands. But if we really believed God was bigger than we were, this was His gift too, and the leap was to trust that He would take care of us no matter the end result.

Sometimes, my friends, realism and faith walk together holding hands, but sometimes they must part ways. It's not forever and not completely so that they lose sight of each other, but it's just enough so that you must choose which one to follow for a time. You will have to feel your way. This is true in all the big and small decisions, from marriage to profession to motherhood to potty training. The answer is not always clear and rarely an all-or-nothing decision, thank the Lord. You will perform extravagant acts and also take rational steps in the path that God has put you on, and He will rejoice in both.

Guiding Questions

1. When have you found yourself holding a give-and-take faith like the disciples?
2. When have you struggled with the silences of God and how have you worked past them?
3. How might you choose to be extravagant with your faith like the woman with the oil? What would be your lavish act?
4. Name one person whose wisdom you seek when you need discernment.

Scripture

- Matthew 26:6–13

Chapter 7

"The Planner" and the Woman at the Well

The beginning of IVF felt a lot like the beginning of teaching. I was given a calendar that did not follow the rhythms of the rest of the world. Just as teachers count down to progress reports and quarter grades and finals, my life was newly marked by fertility idioms such as CD1 (Cycle Day 1) and 1DPO (1 day past ovulation) interspersed with 10 cc X brand estrogen in AM and 10 days of generic steroid tablet in PM (they don't even want to see you with the sniffles during this incubation period). Later in the month, the calendar grew denser, like traveling deeper into the forest. It was populated with items such as 2 vials X estrogen and 150 cc Y follicle-stimulating hormone coupled with specific days to come into the clinic for lab work and/or ultrasounds. It was a reorienting period. Sure, I had been through plenty of medicated cycles with the IUIs, but this was a level I had not imagined. It was the difference between student teaching and getting your own classroom. You're walking the tightrope either with or without a net. Everything rang heavily with importance and responsibility, two of my favorite things.

The Lord knew what He was doing by putting us on this

path as final exams arrived and summer approached. Nothing speaks to a teacher's soul like summer. For me, the truly golden time is the end of May just after exams have been administered, grades turned in, desks cleaned out, and boards wiped down. June is when "real" summer begins, but this is the intro, the prelude, the queueing up of orchestral music before the concert. It's a stolen time to revel in what has been accomplished and survived before moving on to the fun. It is the sorbet between courses, the freshening of the palate. And in this brief week or so before June sprung into being, I stopped to do some thinking.

My thinking was the mental equivalent of flipping back through your planner and taking note of that *one* day you managed to fix yourself a hot breakfast before a 6 a.m. parent-teacher conference, teach three 70-minute classes, eat lunch at your desk while grading quizzes, and swing by the grocery store on your way home so you could cook a "real" dinner. It is a feeling of accomplishment, the satisfaction of tasks checked off the list. I have been known to fill lists with things already done, only for the satisfaction of drawing a neat line through them. It is not sane, but it feels delicious. So, in the May interlude, I stopped and gave myself a minute to think about what we had achieved up to this point. Our marriage had not fallen apart from the stress. We were both still healthy. We were not yet destitute. Jody had gotten a new job that required less travel and I had paradoxically had the best teaching year yet to date. I told myself, as I sat out on our deck with my iced latte and "beach" read that had nothing to do with teaching, that I would remember these things and they would help me take the rest in stride.

The Waiting

During the height of Jesus' notoriety, He traveled back to Galilee by way of Samaria. And because you couldn't just stop at Mapco for snacks, He sent His disciples into the nearest town of Sychar to buy food while He waited by the well. As He was lolling about, a woman approached and He asked her to give Him water. Two things made this request almost unthinkable: (1) Men didn't talk to women alone. It just wasn't done. (2) Samaritans and Jews were not friends. Though technically both from the same stock, the Samaritans came from northern Israel and did not support the rebuilding of Jerusalem by the southern Jews. And the southern Jews definitely did not support the mixed marriages with Gentiles and dabbling in pagan worship that the Samaritans had embraced. Both sides crossed their arms, turned their backs, and refused to shake hands in the schoolyard. It was the butter battle all over again.

This woman at the well had a fighting spirit. She did not shy away from the strange man lurking, as I would, but instead pointed out, "You are a Jew and I am a Samaritan woman. How can you ask me for a drink?" (John 4:9). She was an outcast, alone at the well instead of with the other women. She should have been, if not humble, at least tempered in her conversation. But Jesus didn't take it to heart, and instead steered her toward His point, like a patient driver's ed teacher, subtly turning the wheel. He claimed that He would have given her "living water" (John 4:10) if only she'd asked. But she was a literal woman and balked at His lack of preparation. He carried neither cup nor thermos to hold His catch. That's the frustrating thing about wells. They don't always come with a bucket attached like Jack and Jill's. He tried to push her toward the metaphor so that she could catch it. He said,

"Everyone who drinks this water will be thirsty again, but whoever drinks the water I give him will never thirst" (John 4:13–14). That sold it. She wanted this water that would save her endless time and trips. No more back and forth, embarrassingly alone. This, to her, was a lifesaver, but not in the way Jesus meant. She was at her perfect day in her planner, the one that showed her cruising through life.

But you can't outrun your mistakes or the guilt they cause, no matter how much power you wield. More often than not, when I look back through my planner, the days that stand out are those well-stocked with unchecked "To-Dos." My planner knows my hubris. Apparently, I could not read Chapter 7 of *The Great Gatsby* while on hold with Comcast about our erroneous bill and fold the laundry that had been in the dryer for two days. Moms fall prey to this all the time—too many plates spinning lead to a sea of broken crockery. And then there are the weeks that go by with nothing but blank pages because I'm too busy or too tired to be bothered with it. I couldn't help but notice, too, how Jody and I never went out on "dates" anymore because we didn't have the money or the energy. Who wants to blow-dry their hair when you could just watch *Office Space* again and eat pizza with your swollen feet in the air? I noted all the tailgates or family trips we'd missed because of conflicts with our treatment cycles. And there was that women's retreat at church I skipped this year because I just could not for a minute sit in a circle and share this prayer request or the reams of history behind it. And Netflix beat community group more often than not.

Because I'm *that* girl, I went back farther to all the things I had not done right up to now that could have already messed up this future. I thought back to how I had pushed myself toward total intellectual domination in high school while not fueling myself enough socially, emotionally, or physically. It took an amazing psychologist and nutritionist in college to right my wobbly table that had become so precarious. Who knows what kind of permanent damage I had done in those formative years? My research revealed (because we know I love Google) that cortisol levels increase with stress over a long period of time. They do not settle down easily, kind of like children, actually. My cortisol could be, right now, making my uterus anxious and worrisome so that it twirls its hair and forgets to sleep. That just seemed unfair, a self-sabotage to the nth degree. And despite the fact that all the fertility specialists ensured me that I was in a healthy state, I still feared the repercussions of my past.

My mental planner showed me one thing: I was good at "doing." Despite those odd off days, I was good at setting myself to a task and getting it done. I like my lists crossed off. So once summer was in full swing, I went back to that nutritionist despite the fact that I was supposed to be relaxing my body, mind, and soul, according to our RE. I had her analyze me top to bottom. Was I eating too many sugars? Was I getting enough fat? Should I add more snacks? Fewer snacks? Should I eat more protein? Should I take a supplement of some sort? B vitamins are good for babies, right? I do not know how she put up with me. Except that I must have been profoundly entertaining. I also found a new psychologist to whom I could voice my fears of failure and guilt and the anxiety that I felt was fueling this currently unfruitful state. I rehashed the miscarriage over and over while she listened and handed me

Kleenex. I voiced the quiet dread that I might not even be a good mother while giving myself a hormone injection on her love seat. I brought my own Band-Aids. All these experts told me there was nothing more I could do. They gently ordered me to be nice to myself. But nice worked only for those who could conceive on their honeymoon, sleep past an alarm, and genuinely like bubble baths. I still do not understand baths.

So once again, I took matters into my own hands. I gained extra weight just in case. I took B vitamins labeled STRESS COMPLEX. I doubled my protein intake because babies are made of protein. Jody said I was starting to smell like beef jerky. *C'est la vie.* I saw an acupuncturist, who stuck needles in my forehead, wrists, abdomen, and Achilles tendon. This actually *was* relaxing. I would gladly pay to have someone wrap my feet in a warm blanket, put some soothing music on, turn out the light, and tell me to stay still until the bell *dings*. The places my mind went in those quiet minutes were good most of the time, like daydreaming to the smell of lavender and thyme. I made Jody give me femoral massages every night. This was not as sexy as it sounds. He had to press as hard as he could on my femoral artery at the top of each thigh. Thirty seconds on each side was guaranteed to increase blood flow to the pelvic organs. I was getting things right; all my bases were covered. Just like the woman at the well, I would be practical and prepared to a fault.

Jesus is great at angling life events so we can see past our actions to their causes, like a hair stylist holding up a mirror to your roots. After the woman said, "Sir, give me this water" (John 4:15), He told her to go get her husband. She told Him what He already knew; she had no husband. And so He played

His hand: "The fact is, you have had five husbands, and the man you have now is not your husband" (John 4:17). Believe it or not, having five husbands was not that big of a deal back then. People died a lot, and as you remember from Naomi, it was the responsibility of the deceased husband's family to step up and marry the widows. But living out of wedlock with a man *was* a serious deal. This was not a five-miles-over-the-speed-limit infraction. This was reckless driving. But a sin is a sin is a sin in God's eyes, and this woman's sin was not her lack of a wedding ring; it was pride. Yes, she had to go alone to the well because the other women would have nothing to do with her, but at least she was making her life work on her terms. She was not starving and out on the street. She did not need a Jesus, a savior, because she thought she was saving herself. Hey, that's my trick. Jesus showed her that He wanted to help her anyway, that her life was not working at its full capacity. He wanted more for her. He would keep her company at the well for the rest of her life if she'd let Him.

My conceit had made me self-sufficient. It was what drove me to fill in any possible gap in the baby-making process. Despite how peaceful those acupuncture sessions were, after the bell dinged and the lights came on, everything came whooshing back. I still had to admit that it was my lack of faith in God's goodness that drove me to such measures. It wasn't that the RE or nutritionist or psychologist or acupuncturist was wrong in what they advised. I could engage in self-care, take the drugs, gain the weight, feel all the feels, stimulate the nerves . . . or not. It would still be God creating the life. But I didn't trust Him. All evidence seemed to point to a God who still saw all my errors and was making me pay for them.

It was an odd state in which to live. I believed Jesus had died for all the sins I could and couldn't name and I had known God's grace. But I just hadn't felt the love lately. I was beyond the revival spiritual high. No hymn or hallelujah was going to get me there. God was going to have to be blunt. Nobody can catch themselves from a free fall, and IVF was going to be just that: a free fall into a space where I had no control. And if I'm honest, motherhood is that. A sky dive into unknown territory where your shoot won't open until the very last possible second, and only when someone else pulls the cord.

I know you want to feel the love just as much as I do. I know you want to be at the well right next to Jesus so you can see every pore and hear every compassionate word. I know this is especially true when you're feeling vulnerable, which is exactly what infertility and motherhood do to us. It's hard not to fill up on fluff and busyness. But my prayer is that you choose to stay vulnerable and thirsty for God even when you can't lean over the well and touch Him.

Guiding Questions

1. What does a "good" day in the planner look like to you? What's a "bad" one? How can you rip off the labels?
2. How could you choose vulnerability over self-sufficiency like Jesus asks of the woman at the well?
3. What is one small way God has shown you His love today?

Scripture

- John 4:1–26

Chapter 8

"The Matters of the Heart" and Sarah

My dear friends, I cannot believe we have made it this far and I have not yet brought Sarah, Abraham's wife, to the table. After all, doesn't she kind of stand up as the archetypal infertile woman of the Bible? Her devotion to her husband and to God led not just to fertility but, more important, the blessing of baby Isaac. Her actions and faith merited the title of "the mother of nations" (Genesis 17:16). I always pictured her as a matronly grandmother with hair falling in a braid down her back, hands covered in flour from kneading dough. Apparently, my Sarah is a frontierswoman. She could have traveled the Oregon Trail. I love Sarah for what she represents: a promise fulfilled by God to a woman in desperate need of a Hail Mary as the clock runs down. And I love her for all the things she did wrong, just as much as all she got right. She is my patron saint of mothers for her flaws.

Sarah wasn't always old and dowdy. Before she was Sarah, she was "Sarai" and she was stunning. There was a famine in the land as was the fashion of the times, so Abraham (still "Abram" at this point) and Sarai moved to Egypt until the crops could grow and he could return home to Bethel. Now Sarai must have been a knockout, the kind of gorgeous that

Scarlett Johansson and Sophia Vergas have—they draw men like moths to a flame. Abram was convinced that the minute they passed through customs, the Egyptians would want her for their own. He feared they'd kill him to get her. What's another moth sacrificed to the cause? So he hatched a plan: "Say you are my sister, so that I will be treated well for your sake and my life will be spared because of you" (Genesis 12:13). Guys always try to buddy up to the pretty girl's brother.

He must have studied up on his Egyptians fairly well, because everything he predicted came to pass, and when Pharaoh got wind of Sarai's beauty, he had her brought to live in the palace. Abram did not put up much of a fight. He was busy accumulating "sheep and cattle, male and female donkeys, menservants and maidservants, and camels" (12:16) as part of the exchange. What do you think those whispered snatches of conversations looked like between husband and wife in the corridors of the palace? Do you think Sarai was A-okay with the plan, checking in on how much livestock they were tallying, or do you think she was adding it all up in her head as an unpardonable crime Abram would pay for later? Probably a little bit of both. Despite their success, it was never going to end well. So, when Pharaoh and his entourage suffered a plague of diseases from flying too close to another man's wife, Pharaoh banished the two. "Take her and go!" he said and pushed them out the door (Genesis 12:19). They pulled this same stunt later with another king, Abimelech. They had found their niche.

The Bible doesn't get specific about when in their marriage Sarai and Abram figured out that she couldn't have kids, but it must have been pretty quick because the first time she appears in Genesis, she's introduced as "barren" (Genesis 11:29). Who knows how long they tried before giving up? But eventually, they did. And with the force of her acrimony, she told her husband, "The Lord has kept me from having children. Go, sleep with my maidservant; perhaps I can build a family through her" (Genesis 16:2). There was an element of practicality to all this. God had already foretold that "a son coming from your own body will be your heir" (Genesis 15:4) when Abram complained that the servants would have to claim his inheritance in absentia. Sarai was going to get him that baby one way or another. Don't we all feel that at some point with our wants? Whatever it is, if it does not arrive on schedule, the prayers slow and the actions increase.

Becoming a mother was like that for me. We examined each of our options in desperate measure. Drugs, shots, surgeries, donors, surrogates, adoption. Acupuncture, prayer, protein, vitamins, massage, hymns. No stone was left unturned. Sarai did the same thing. She took matters into her own hands and Abram didn't put up much of a fight. She handed over Hagar to be put to good use. Sarai's action plan worked. Hagar conceived in a jiffy and thus we have Ishmael. But when we try to do things in our own way, in our own time, the results within our hearts will not be the same as if we had let God show us the way.

For me, the worry and the panicky action muddied the water and made the process much more stressful than it needed to be. I'd lost my mission statement. What was I doing all this for? How many mothers have felt that—that they've lost sight of the thing they once knew they wanted with all their heart?

Imagine Sarai at this point. She was still beautiful, but probably beginning to show signs of wear and tear: a few graying hairs, creases around the mouth and eyes she could no longer claim were laugh lines. And she watched her servant grow rounder and rosier as the gestational weeks turned into months and Hagar's position in the household grew exponentially. Then Ishmael arrived, a screaming bundle of reality of which Sarai could not partake. And Hagar wasn't shy in flaunting her success. She was a first-time mother, still marveling at the miracle of life. The sheen hadn't yet worn off and she didn't care if it maddened her mistress. But unlike Hannah, who stopped eating and wept copiously when Peninnah taunted her, Sarai pointed a finger at Abram saying, "You are responsible for the wrong I am suffering ... May the Lord judge between you and me" (Genesis 16:5). They were such a pair, weren't they? I bet their fights were loud and fierce and full of broken pottery. But this time Abram relented, threw up his hands, and gave Hagar to Sarai to do with as she pleased—which was as ominous as it sounds. Our Sarai became a bully who forced Hagar to flee with Ishmael. This was the matriarch of the Jewish people? A promise had been fulfilled. The heritage had begun. But Sarai's heart was off-kilter.

I remember that IVF summer as the hottest on record. The world was a mirage of heat waves, tired cicadas, browning grass, and panting dogs. I was always out of breath and puffy in weird places from water retention. How do the tops of your toes gain weight? There were no moths gravitating toward my flame. I was a hot mess. I walked the aisles at Target hiding granny-style compression socks under my skirt. Target was my best friend in those days. It offered air-conditioning on full blast and at least an hour's worth of distraction from the rest of my life. This would be true later in the mothering years. Target is every woman's best friend—it is always there in times of crisis with its Cartwheel sales and scented candles. I also drank liters of water and ate all the Sonic Oreo Blasts because whole milk is good for building a hospitable womb and soul. I endured the heat like I had endured everything else—head down and shoulders set. I would catch myself imagining some sort of sainthood because of all this. The constant hardship would rub me clean, leaving me shiny like a new penny. Mary and Sarah and Hannah and all the other mothers in the Bible would welcome me into their club with soft golf claps and a cup of tea.

Sarah clearly didn't have her act together at this point. She was a beautiful woman who knew how to use beauty to her advantage. She had grown used to getting her own way and was mercilessly jealous and petulant when it didn't work out. She was also disrespectful to the point of blasphemy when she heard God tell Abraham, "I will surely return to you about this time next year, and Sarah your wife will have a son" (Genesis 18:10). She laughed to herself and muttered snarkily, "After I am worn out and my master is old, will I now have this pleasure?" (Genesis 18:12). God had sentenced people to silence and leprosy for less than this. And then she lied, like a kid who just stuck his toothbrush in the toilet but thinks no one will be the wiser. What? Who me? God, in His best dad voice, said, "Yes, you did laugh" (Genesis 18:15), when she denied it. *It's written all over your face, Sarah.*

Much like Sarah, I was not ready to cede this match to

God just yet. My heart refused to budge. But somehow God works around us. Sarai did become Sarah, whose name means "noblewoman." Despite her deceptions and her laughter, "the Lord was gracious to Sarah as he had said, and the Lord did what he had promised. Sarah became pregnant and bore a son to Abraham in his old age, at the very time God had promised him" (Genesis 21:1–2). Imagine, if you will, the swirling force of nature that Sarah must have been while in the throes of premenopausal pregnancy and mood swings. Even after Isaac, she fell back into old patterns. She feared Ishmael would outshine her boy and went so far as to demand that Abraham banish Hagar and her son. Lucky for us, God can still use the stubborn ones for His purposes. We are the cats clawing at every surface so as not to go in the bath. Even though a good scrubbing is precisely what we need.

It's a bit harder to picture Sarah as a dignified mother to the nations when you review her rap sheet, but it is vital to remember as you walk through your own wilderness. In this purgatorial summer, God did not wait for me to act a certain way or learn my lesson in order to let me conceive. Thank goodness.

He does not need you to get yourself right before He acts. He is bigger than your attitudes. He will use your circumstances for your good and His glory no matter what. However, to practice trust and to pay attention to the heart when all you want to do is shut it down in the name of action might be the most refining part of the process. Doing is not always better. Stillness is a virtue too. My learning of this lesson came later.

Guiding Questions

1. When has God changed your circumstances for good despite your attitude?
2. What is one way you can practice stillness and trust over action today?

Scripture

- Genesis 11:29, 12:10–20, 15:5, 16:1–16, 17:15–16, 18:10–15

Chapter 9

"The Unexpected" and Hagar in the Desert

Remember those boxes of needles and syringes and medications and bandages and swabs dragged in from the carport and lined up like little soldiers on the countertop? If a medicated IUI is sending in the army to fight infertility, IVF is the army, navy, marines, and air force all fighting dirty. We were in the jungle swinging from the vines, hitting it from all sides.

Deep in the middle of the sweaty armpit that was that hot summer, I was ordered by my job to unwind, get outside, stick my feet in the pool, and forget what day it was. And yet, I was tethered to the clock. It was a great deal like being a mother actually. You dream of soaking up the sun and lying in a raft with a cocktail but instead lifeguard your kids in a grandma swimsuit and count the minutes until naptime. I gave myself two shots in the belly in the morning. One of them looked like a fat pen. It even had a click top. I picked it up once to write a check. Evenings called for one pill and yet another shot. It was such an odd feeling, that cold refrigerated liquid dissolving through my body. In between all of this was the morning hot water with lemon juice to alkalize the body and the Brazil nuts for selenium and the eggs, eggs, and more eggs for protein. I had fallen down the rabbit hole. By nightfall, my purse held little baggies of used syringes and Band-Aids and eggshells.

The IVF calendar was all-knowing and all-reaching and overshadowed any kind of plans for late nights out. I had to be home to give myself the refrigerated shot, and big as my hobo bag was, I wasn't about to carry a mini cooler. Gone were the days of a glass of wine with dinner. And possibly worst of all, no more coffee. Coffee and I have a special relationship. Coffee gives me something that Jody cannot. Coffee says to me with that first creamy sip, you can do this; let's tackle this day together. Without it, I was merely an empty vessel with a raging headache. This is my most poignant sensory memory from those months: trudging through the sweltering days with puffy feet and a headache that predictably and masochistically increased as the day wore on. By nightfall, it was incapacitating. I whispered this mantra to myself in the dark: "It's only temporary."

After weeks of injections, the ultrasound and blood work visits began. Everything was minutely measured and every measurement was critical. Imagine, if you will, trying to balance your ovaries in the very center of a seesaw, which is perched on a trampoline. This was tricky business. I was in that office enough to hone my clinic persona. I was the jokester with the nurses taking blood. They see dozens an hour. My goal was to make them look up just once. I told the kind of jokes you'd find on Popsicle sticks. I was the penitent with the ultrasound technicians. Probing questions about what's on the screen are forbidden because it is against protocol, so I tried to behave. Lastly, I was the mimic with the doctor. You run off their cues. If they're chatty, you're chatty. If they're terse, you're mute.

When you sign over your life to IVF, you are given a special voice mail and password only you can access, which will expire at the end of your treatment like the letter in spy movies you must burn after reading. This chain of numbers becomes your lifeline. It holds the key to your day's activities, your mood, and your course for subsequent days. Much like regular motherhood, your schedule is no longer your own. I'd handed over the keys. After clinic visits, a nurse would leave me a voice mail late in the day with my results. This determined what dosage of medicine I would give myself until the next visit and when that next visit would be. Lucky for me, they could not tell how many times in an afternoon I'd check this voice mail. It was borderline manic. But I knew that if I had any concerns or confusion about my instructions, I only had until the end of office hours to get someone to call me back. Otherwise, you're ringing the on-call doctor, which is not cool if it's not an emergency. You don't want to be *that* lady.

My attitude during all this? Despite the physical discomfort and the thousands of unknowns, I was surprisingly calm . . . or numb, one of the two. I thought that everything up until now had inured me for this season. Or perhaps it was not having to work. Or perhaps it was all the "doing" I was doing to make everything work out. Or perhaps it was simply God giving me a rest before the downhill slide into what would come next. Regardless, things went swimmingly. At my final appointment, I had twenty-six eggs ripe for the picking. For fun, let's do some math. If a woman ovulates a traditional twelve times a year, releasing one egg per ovulation cycle, how many months would she have to ovulate to get twenty-six eggs? That's right. I grew over two years' worth of eggs in six weeks. My basket was full to the brim.

We need to revisit Hagar for a minute. Hagar always gets the rough end of the story. She is somehow reduced to a side note, a time filler until Sarah conceived Isaac. Ishmael is just a stray offshoot on the family tree. But the Bible implies no such thing. Look at the text: "Sarai his wife took her Egyptian maidservant Hagar and *gave her* to her husband to be his wife" (Genesis 16:3). Sarah handed her over. Hagar became his wife. She took up a position in the household and the hereditary line that cannot and should not be forgotten. And with that lineage came more conflict.

After her conception, she began to "despise her mistress" (Genesis 16:4). In fairness to Hagar, it had to have been hard to play second fiddle to Sarah. Going from servant to wife would be a bumpy adjustment for all parties. This is why interoffice relationships are never a good idea.

After she became a wife but before she was pregnant, she suffered so much abuse from her former mistress that she made a run for it. Yet God did not forget Hagar. An angel of the Lord found her sitting by a stream in the desert. He sent her back with a promise: "I will so increase your descendants that they will be too numerous to count" (Genesis 16:10). He was the world's most accurate pregnancy test. "You are now with child, and you will have a son. You shall name him Ishmael, for the Lord has heard of your misery" (Genesis 16:11), he said. Hagar returned, submitted, and had Ishmael. This Egyptian slave woman became the mother to a nation.

I felt more like Hagar than Sarah when listening to that

nurse over voice mail report my dozens of eggs and tell me the appointed hour to shoot the shot that would release my hatchlings. I was blessed beyond belief at my windfall, totally shocked by my move up in the world. When Jody heard the numbers, he went mute for half a day to process. He would have gone longer, but he had only a limited amount of time to get it together before surgery the following day. Our eggs would be ushered off to the lab so they could meet their new best friends, the sperm, provided Jody did his job. We had backup in the freezer just in case. This is IVF. They leave nothing to chance.

The next morning after my last "relaxation" session of acupuncture and just two days before the Fourth of July, we drove to the clinic in jittery silence and entered a door that had always been barred to us: the wing to the surgery center. Oddly, the room they put me in before surgery had the same painting, a deep purple iris, as my IUI room. I wondered, briefly, if that was good or bad luck. I don't remember much of the time from pre- to post-egg retrieval. I was following Gene Wilder down a trippy tunnel in the Chocolate Factory and would need just a minute to recoup upon waking to find Jody, still in his hospital-issued blue hat and scrubs. He looked like a Smurf doctor. The surgery had gone well, he whispered, as I squinted one eye and then the other at him. All the eggs were off to the lab to be greeted by a welcome wagon of embryologists.

It was the most ethereal I had ever felt, most likely the lingering kiss of the anesthesia. The relief was exquisite because, for the moment, my job was done. All I had to do was rest, and then go home to rest some more. Everyone kept telling me I had done great, like it was the end of a marathon. Of course, we all knew the real finish line was after the embryo transfer. This would take place in three to five days, after the eggs and sperm had a chance to be fruitful and multiply.

While we waited for our discharge papers, Jody played U2 on his phone because we were headed to their concert the following night. Freedom at last. Bring out the band! We talked about the next few days and generally reveled in the crossing of our Rubicon, or at least one of its tributaries. When I was released, I was in some pain. It was nothing excruciating, kind of like a balloon inflating in my abdomen, a mild pressure from the inside out. I chocked it up to the fact that I had just had minor surgery, popped a few pain pills, and went to bed. It was the first night in months I did not have to wake to use the bathroom. I would come to find out later, when it was too late, that this was a bad omen.

The downside to Hagar's impeccable fertility and mothering of Ishmael was that she still had to live with Sarah. Remember, God ordered her to "Go back to your mistress and submit to her" (Genesis 16:9). And even after Sarah had Isaac and should therefore have no reason to resent Hagar, she asked Abraham to "get rid of that slave woman and her son, for that slave woman's son will never share in the inheritance with my son Isaac" (Genesis 21:10). Abraham regretfully sent her and Ishmael away but only after being assured by God that they would be looked after. *Here's some food and water, Hagar; best of luck to you and my firstborn son.* What a horrific scene that must have been. And she went and she walked and watched as the water ran dry and her son developed the telltale signs of dehydration. How much water do you think she withheld from herself before she finally hid him under a bush and succumbed to delirium, sobbing and saying to herself, "I cannot watch the boy die" (Genesis 21:16)?

Why does it seem like you never get enough time to enjoy a blessing before trouble comes nosing its way in the door? Hagar would become a wife, but would suffer Sarah's wrath. Hagar would get Ishmael, but feel the sting of Sarah's jealousy. Hagar would beget an entire people, but not before watching her son begin to die in the desert of Beersheba.

It has become a self-preservation tactic for me over the years to look for danger even in the brightest spot of sunshine. Great teaching schedule this year? They must be setting me up to sponsor the Honor Society. Jody's new job panning out well? The insurance probably isn't as good. Slept well last night? I'm probably getting mono. I rarely let myself enjoy the good things for fear of the bad.

On this one occasion, after the egg retrieval, I went home and tried thinking only good things for the future. But when I woke up the following morning looking five months' pregnant and in so much pain it was hard to stand, my first thought was: *Yeah, that's about right.*

Please, please don't be me in this. Self-preservation works only if you're at the controls. If you're a worrier like me, give yourself the grace to sit in the sun without looking for shadows and bracing for disappointment. Let yourself enjoy the ups without bracing for the downs. Because, yes, the downs will come this side of heaven, but they do not have to override all the rest.

Guiding Questions

1. When have you caught yourself questioning your good circumstances?
2. How might you practice living a more optimistic life regardless of your situation?

Scripture

- Genesis 16:1–16, 21:8–16

Chapter 10

"The Unwell" and Hagar and the Crippled Woman's Rescue

I drove Jody to the U2 concert the following night, dropping him off at the intersection of a school playground and the children's hospital. This was as close to downtown as I could get. Groups of friends were waiting blocks away. That's how epic this concert was going to be. Parts of the city had been closed off, seemingly at random, and the streets hummed with a pre-apocalyptic hysteria. Pedestrians wandered into the road at unpredictable intervals, and cars parked on curbs with abandon. The policemen stuck to script and attempted to direct the increasingly aggressive traffic. It seemed like the entire city had a date with Bono. Meanwhile, I went home and curled up in the Adirondack chair on the deck to listen to the cicadas scream. Looking back, Jody still cannot believe he went to the concert without me. He shakes his head like a man waking from a dream. But the thing is, we didn't know what was happening to me. We still thought this was typical post-op pain, despite the fact that I could barely walk. Despite the fact that the stretchy pants that fit yesterday did not fit today. Despite the fact that I was having trouble catching my breath and couldn't stomach a full meal. We were in the zone. This was the IVF go-big-or-go-home final leg of the race.

The nurse had called my secret agent voice mail that morning to tell me that we had nine healthy top-notch embryos. *Nine.* Nine potential babies that God had placed in the warming drawer were awaiting our arrival. The plan was to freeze seven and use the top two for the transfer. It was just two days away. We had switched doctors at the beginning of the IVF process because we had not felt the old one was particularly invested in us. She never really remembered us from one appointment to the next. She was typically late and never seemed to have done her homework before showing up to a meeting. I'd never let a student get away with that kind of performance. We typically spent ten silent minutes staring at the top of her head while she read over the notes of all that had occurred in the canyon-sized gaps between our visits with her. She also usually called me Jody. It's a common mistake, but you'd like the doctor in charge of your future to be good with the details.

Our new RE was a short gray-haired man whom I instantly fell in "like" with. He had wit and warmth. He could appreciate the *New York Times* cartoon in ways that made me wish we were friends in real life. And he genuinely cared what happened to us. He even, gasp, asked me how I was holding up when we met with him. This man was thrilled with our news of nine embryos, shocked a little as most were, for we seemed to be beating the odds on this one for once. It was almost unheard of, like winning the lottery twice or updating your iPhone without a glitch. So we assumed the hard part was behind us and all that was left was the gentle coast into parenthood. When I suggested that Jody go to the concert without me, I wasn't really playing the martyr. It was okay by me, because I was protecting our future. It felt bigger than Bono. Plus, I couldn't really stand up at all, which might pose a problem at the venue.

Sometime during the evening, as I watched the last of the daylight fall into darkness, the pain became unbearable. I could barely get myself up to move inside. Like an arthritic, I took it in small hitching steps. This was far beyond tears and codeine. By the time Jody came home, still humming the last lines of "Running to Stand Still," he found me curled in the middle of our bed whispering to myself that it was going to be okay and rocking back and forth like the girl from "The Yellow Wallpaper." This would not have been a good advertisement for IVF. We paged our new RE and told him how I was really holding up.

He was concerned but calm when I hobbled in the next morning in a giant muumuu dress and compression socks with no shoes. The swelling had gotten so bad that I would have worn full body compression gear if such a thing existed. It would be the opposite of a Snuggie and it would keep me together. There are certain standard vitals that must be taken every time you come in, regardless of the reason for your visit. My temperature was normal. My blood pressure was a bit high. And my weight? Up eight pounds in two days. Odd, I thought, was there a baby in there I didn't know about? Our RE did an ultrasound and showed me a picture of my insides that looked like nothing I'd ever seen before. Apparently, I *had* been growing something, but it wasn't a baby. It was a lake. A big swirling mass of liquid had pooled right in the

middle of my "third space." This space, in case you are wondering, is basically any spot in your body under the skin that
is not taken up by organs. In the Milton Bradley game "Oper-
ation," this is all the space your tweezers can't go . . . because
it's supposed to be boring there. This is the desert where nothing grows, unless you're me and call down the floods.

There's something lurking in all the waivers and financial
agreements and medication labels. It's a potential outcome of
IVF that Jody and I never fully registered because it affected
such a small percentage of people, like the allergy medication
that may or may not cause paralysis. My "potential compli-
cation" was ovarian hyperstimulation syndrome. We'll call
it what the cool kids call it: OHSS. This happens when the
body overdoses on estrogen (all those shots). When the eggs
are removed from the follicles during egg retrieval, the ovaries keep pumping out fluid to heal the holes, like a wound
that oozes and then scabs. But mine weren't scabbing. Vascu-
lar hyperpermeability essentially means lots and lots of liquid
going places it doesn't belong. It was a volcano spewing lava
that never hardened. I was molten.

There are three different levels to OHSS: mild, moderate,
and severe. Mild includes bloating, nausea, and some weight
gain. Moderate includes weight gain of more than two pounds
a day, rounding of the stomach from the bloating (pregnancy
belly), and excessive thirst with little urine output. Lots of
drinking, little peeing. I was in the moderate category. As my
RE proceeded to heft me onto the examination table and perform a vaginal tap to relieve the pressure, I decided I did not
want to be his friend after all. You can never go back from this.

A vaginal tap is exactly what it sounds like. Think back

to your college days and imagine a keg being tapped, but instead of a keg, it's a uterus. With just a hose, a needle, and a few glass beakers, you, too, can ferment your own brew. The pain was excruciating, but the relief was profound. It was like finally finding a rest stop after hundreds of miles on a car trip, but exponentially better. He extracted two liters of fluid into glass jars that looked, I kid you not, like growlers. And then he told me to go eat a huge meal because this is the emptiest I would feel for a while. The problem with OHSS is that it continues. These follicles, turned cysts, don't wind down easily. They just keep pumping out the fluid. They are the overachievers in spin class. But he hadn't voiced my worst fears just yet, so I didn't let myself worry. He hadn't called off the transfer. So Jody and I went and ate steak and fries at three in the afternoon and didn't talk about possibilities.

The Bible does not say how much time passed for Hagar as she wandered in the desert and parceled out water. We do not know how long it was after her sobs turned to dry heaves and her boy's wails grew to whimpers before an angel appeared to her and pointed out a well of water. Was it hours or days or weeks before the suffering was relieved and the angel said, "What is the matter, Hagar? Do not be afraid; God has heard the boy crying as he lies there. Lift the boy up and take him by the hand, for I will make him into a great nation" (Genesis 21:17–18)? Time is relative when you or the ones you love are in the middle of an emergency. The first year of motherhood can often feel like this too: 365 days of crisis. It is why first birthdays look like hipster weddings and make everybody cry.

One fine Sabbath as Jesus was teaching in one of the synagogues, He healed a woman who had been crippled by an evil spirit for eighteen years. She was "bent over and could not straighten up at all" (Luke 13:11). She did not approach Him or grab at Him like the woman who bled for twelve years. She had come to listen, perhaps not wanting to call attention to herself. She just wanted to hear what this great man had to say. But He saw her and called her to Him. Picture how slow and agonizing that walk must have been as she passed the curious or impatient temple goers, who whispered and stared. But, oh, the reward when He said, "Woman, you are set free from your infirmity" (Luke 13:12) and put His hands on her and she stood up tall for the first time in almost two decades. You can't get that kind of deep stretch in yoga. Of course, this was prime fodder for the rulers, who took issue with miracles on the Sabbath. Marvels were for business days only. Do you think they also had working hours? Jesus loved to pick at the nitpickers. He responded to their disapproval with this: "You hypocrites! Doesn't each of you on the Sabbath untie your ox or donkey from the stall and lead it out to give it water?" (Luke 13:15). If they could care for animals on the Sabbath, how could He ignore "a daughter of Abraham" (Luke 13:16)? Like Hagar and the crippled woman, when the time was right, the healing would come, but not a moment before.

I did not know when my ovaries would seal up and my body would find normalcy, but I prayed for it to happen in the next twenty-four hours. We had an appointment the following day when my RE would make the final call. This was the best attempt at living in the moment that I had done up to that point. You can't get much more grateful for the little things than when you are thanking God for French fries and pee breaks. My relief, however, was short-lived. When I woke up the following morning, I couldn't sit up straight again and, more disconcertingly, couldn't seem to catch my breath. This one, they said, meant, *Do not stop, do not pass Go, get yourself immediately to the clinic.* They meant you should have someone else drive you there, because hyperventilating is worse than texting when it comes to operating a vehicle. I ignored that part. I cannot adequately describe both the humor and the horror of the conversation I had with the head of the English department while barreling down the interstate and explaining in very short bursts of breath that I would not be able to make it to that day's in-service. She calmly told me to hang up the phone and get to the hospital. They would carry on with the computer training without me.

The nurse at the front desk took one look at me and shooed me through to the back. I was wearing the muumuu again and had draped a purple fleece blanket embroidered with my school's insignia over my shoulders. I looked like a huge toddler. I think they feared what the sight of me would do to the couples holding hands and watching CNBC in the waiting room.

It's amazing how you can be severely dehydrated while retaining up to thirty pounds of water. Because that's what the results showed—I had gained thirty pounds in three days. It took two sticks in both arms before they could start an IV. My veins were just empty. They did another tap, this one more painful than the last, and got three more liters, but there was no relief, because what the ultrasound showed this time was that fluid had now entered my abdomen, crowded my internal organs into a tiny protective huddle, and wormed its way into my lungs. With pleural effusion and respiratory distress, I had now reached level three: severe.

The Waiting

You can't drain fluid from the abdomen or the lungs with a vaginal tap for obvious reasons. You can't leave the office and eat a steak an hour later either and you certainly can't transfer an embryo into the churning ocean. The transfer was off. Into the freezer you go, my babes. They prepared a room and admittance for me in the adjacent hospital. As I lay shivering on my side on the examination table waiting for Jody to arrive, I thought of nothing. I did not think about the pain or the new calendar or the money or the past. I lay there and counted breaths, trying and failing to make them last longer. It was breath-by-breath living. My body and my mind had stopped speaking to each other.

I don't know if Hagar prayed while she cried or if the crippled woman still argued with her demon tormentor or if they both had ceased hoping and entered that state of existence that is not living but is not yet death. It would take an anesthetized abdominal tap of seven liters of fluid. It would take two lung taps, the medical version of a hammer chiseling a needle through my back and between my ribs, to reach the liquid. It would take four hospitalized days on oxygen. It would take all this before my body began to heal. Despite having all the time in the world, I still did not think. Mild pain sharpens the senses and the mind. Stub your toe and the world explodes in stars and colorful expletives. But severe, long-lasting pain numbs. There is no adrenaline left to pump. I lay there while my insides burbled, and I breathed in and out and watched the blinking of machines and listened to the whir of oxygen and wondered, with a detached curiosity, what was going to happen next.

There really is no difference between Hagar and the crippled woman despite their different approaches to God. These stories from the Bible are not a master index of what to do and what not to do to get God to finally listen to you. These women, me included, exist to share how God did it in our tiny bubble so that you can know there are others out there with the same hurts and losses and fears. The rulers of the synagogue were always looking for the angle, trying to work the system in their favor, because they couldn't see from a higher elevation. Other women's stories serve to remind me that I am still part of the picture. My little happenings, when pooled together with theirs and yours, make it feel more bearable and remind me that my timeline has already panned out. I just can't see it. Wishful mothers, new mothers, old mothers, we're all in it together. And sometimes all you really need is time to get a good look at it. Even if it's the last thing you want.

Guiding Questions

1. When have you found yourself impatient with God's timing?
2. How can you practice patience while you wait for God to work?
3. What is one promise that God has already fulfilled in your life?
4. What pieces of your story might help other women redefine their expectations and find hope?

Scripture

- Genesis 21:17–20
- Luke 13:11–16

Chapter 11

"The Calm Waters" and Noah's Wife

Genesis often reads like something out of *Lord of the Rings* in its far-sweeping scope of the state of the kingdom. You can almost hear Sir Ian McKellen narrating the "wickedness of the human race" (Genesis 6:5). We were creatures of the sixth day, and we had forgotten our charge. God was "grieved that he made man on earth and his heart was filled with pain" (Genesis 6:6). So He said, "I will wipe out mankind, whom I have created, from the face of the earth—men and animals, and creatures that move along the ground, and birds of the air" (Genesis 6:7).

We all know this story, for we owe our continued existence to one man: Noah. The Bible says, "Noah was a righteous man, blameless among the people of his time, and he walked with God" (Genesis 6:9). Now let us all transport back to Sunday school and the felt board where fuzzy animals marched two-by-two on their wobbly journey to the ark. And let us all picture the huge behemoth of a boat stuck up in the corner at right angles. Even in felt it had a certain ceremonial quality to it, didn't it? Noah proceeded under orders to "bring into the ark two of all living creatures, male and female" (Genesis 6:19). Load them up and ship them out.

But Noah is not the focus of our story here. I want to talk about Mrs. Noah. God said to him, "But I will establish my covenant with you, and you will enter the ark—you and your sons and your wife and your sons' wives with you" (Genesis 6:18). She was the nameless one, the one after the dash and sandwiched between conjunctions. We get to know the boys a bit later, Shem, Ham, and Japheth. But Noah's wife seems vague. She's the felt cutout that's so generic no one can place it. It keeps falling off the board. Was her experience any less? She felt the heaving of the boat over those waves. She fed the animals and took out the trash. She cooked the meals and walked the dog and did what she could to keep the family afloat. Yet she lacked any real personality. She'd be "Wife of Noah" in the film credits. Her placement on the periphery became significant, though, as I recovered from my own flood.

I do not have an hourglass figure. The small frame that worked to my advantage in high school in cross-country and on the tennis court was a disadvantage in child-birthing years. Try as I might, I could never exchange my ruler for pear. Genetics is a powerful thing. But when I stood for the first time in the hospital room after my illness, after the oxygen was disconnected, the machines silenced, the IVs removed, and the wounds bandaged, I saw something entirely against protocol. From the top up, I looked like me, maybe a little tired and greasy from four days without a real shower, but still me. But from the waist down I was the funhouse version of a Kardashian. Despite having lost half of the extra fluid by this point, my thighs and legs were thick sausages, packed tight and slightly purple. In fact, I could hardly bend my legs at all. The crease at the back of the knee had become inverted.

The Waiting

The hospital room mirror was a tiny square, showing only my upper half, so when I looked down, the view was disorienting, a personal vertigo. They assured me this was normal when I had to send Jody home a second time for the one pair of gaucho pants I could maneuver over my hips. Our new RE—the poor man had visited multiple times a day, even on his days off—explained the process in fine detail: As the fluid leaves the body, it follows gravity. I should expect frequent urination as the swelling travels southward. Buy some Gatorade. Eat more jerky. They all thought my jerky habit was hilarious. But in the coming weeks, protein, salt, and hydration would be my trifecta. I sat and listened and tried to wiggle my fat toes. This little piggy cried, "Wee wee wee!" The stretch marks from that one week of expansion and then deflation are a cartographer's dream, a precise map of my journey to motherhood. They say pregnancy does a number on your body, but for me, getting there was the real mind meld.

Slowly, the doctor said, I would come back to myself, when they let me finish the healing process at home. Once I was released back into the wild, I reveled in my freedom, taking the dog on short and then increasingly longer walks. You should have seen me toddling along down the avenue. I drank the Gatorade with my feet up in bed and began the lesson plans that would kick off yet another year of teaching. I grilled salmon and huge juicy hamburgers, celebrating the fact that my stomach had room to fill. And toward the end of this month, the July to end all Julys, I appeared mostly back to my old self. Which was exactly how I did not want to look. Because by now I wanted to look pregnant.

Jody and I got the call late one evening after I'd been home a few weeks. We had been sitting out on the back deck in the dark during the only time of the day it was cool enough to do so. I remember it being a quiet night, only fireflies and a few crickets to break the solitude. The phone buzzed with the news that Jody's sister was in labor and would probably have the baby sometime in the night or the following morning. Because this was the first grandchild on his side and we were attachment-free, we made plans to drive over the next day.

The three hours in the car passed largely in small talk with our brother-in-law's brother and wife, who were hitching a ride to meet the new baby. I remember coffee and bagels and propping my feet up on the dash because they still tended to swell if I sat for too long. I remember the skirt I was wearing; it had elephants on it, marching across my thighs in an endless circle. This was the baby that had been in the works when we all started trying at the same time. This was the baby whose shower I attended not long after my miscarriage. This little baby was now a fully formed person. How could I still be shocked that this happened to people?

And after many hand washings and sanitizings and stepping in and out of the room so the new mom could be checked and resituated, we finally met the little guy. He was so tiny, which was natural, being born five weeks early (she had had her own dose of drama with this one), but he was the cutest little dark-haired dude. I held him, most of his girth explained away by the blanket that cocooned him. The duality of this moment is hard to express and best captured in a picture I came across later. It shows me sitting in a rocking chair draped in a hospital gown with my head tilted down toward this new life. I look stunned. Stunned that he was real and stunned that he was not mine. Happy. Wistful. Hopeful. Sad. It's all there in the photograph.

By the time school started again, I was back on the fertility wagon. But it really didn't feel like it. We were scheduled to do a frozen embryo transfer (FET) in September, and when the box of medications arrived, I thought there'd been a mistake. It was so small. Even the disposable syringe container was smaller. After IVF, anything would have felt like a lessening of intensity, but the prep for this thing was even lower key than the IUIs. My body had already done the hardest work and suffered the consequences by producing all those eggs. And Jody's job was done until a baby popped into the world. He could drink all the beer and tour all the hot tubs in North America. Our nine lives were stashed safely away in a secure facility. There was so little required of us, it almost felt like a letdown, like this would never work for lack of sacrifice.

The most medication I would have to give myself over the course of this FET was right before the transfer and up until the pregnancy test ten days later. These were the estrogen and progesterone intramuscular injections. I had determined that the least painful place to give them was in the fleshy part of my lower back/hip because it offered the easiest access to the biggest muscle. I gave thanks for every bite of Häagen-Dazs, because I needed the biggest square footage possible. These were the beasts of the shot world, needles the size of coffee stirrers. Jody had to do the shooting. I hadn't really wanted someone who was still rubbing the sleep out of his eyes and wearing his shirt inside out to aim a sharp coffee stirrer at my soft spots, but we made do. Such is life.

To adequately prepare for the shot, I would first ice down

the area for two minutes and then shift my weight to the opposite leg. It's why they always tell you to relax your arm before the flu shot. It's also nearly impossible to do. I would stand, as zen as possible in my stork position and Jody would let fly the needle, pulling ever so slightly back on the plunger once it was imbedded to make sure he hadn't hit a vein. And then he'd inject the viscous liquid nice and slow. My husband, who can't finish a meal without some on his shirt, was in charge of this process. But he did it and, to his credit, did it well nine times out of ten.

Noah's wife is mentioned five times in total. She's never named and she's always clustered in with her sons' wives. But she endured 40 days of unrelenting rain and a total of 150 days on a boat with all the animals in the world and all their roarings and brayings and cawings and excrement. And she witnessed the return of the dove with the long-awaited olive branch. And when God tells Noah, "Come out of the ark, you and your wife and your sons and their wives" (Genesis 8:16), she got the same salvation. She, too, looked up into the sky, her sandals still mucky with mud, and witnessed the rainbow, that improbable display of colors against a background of blue. God was speaking to her also when He said, "I have set my rainbow in the clouds, and it will be a sign of my covenant between me and the earth" (Genesis 9:13).

So despite the fact that I had stood witness to my sister-in-law's blessing and still waited for my own, I prayed to catch a bit of the overflow. I taught and went to acupuncture and the movies and the bank, and life carried on. Jody and I cruised through all six seasons of *Lost* (again) and drank some wine. And then, one morning as the leaves were lightening with the first hints of yellow and ginger, we drove back to the clinic, where two embryos were just beginning to wake from their frozen daze. Jody donned his Smurf gear and I popped the prescribed Valium (happy uterus equals happy baby), and we watched on a screen as these two fledglings went home to roost in what we prayed would be a long-term lease on my uterus. There was (almost) too much cupped in this moment for me to feel anything at all. I was both ready and not ready to be perched here with my feet in stirrups and my cold hand holding on to Jody's for dear life. Motherhood seemed like such a long way to fall without a net.

The wait is longer for some than others. Noah's wife waited those 150 days for signs of life on the still waters, and she stolidly held out the same hope and said the same prayers as her husband. She is the one I like to honor because I had often felt like a spectator in my own life. I had watched myself get sick and get well and I had watched others grow and give birth and I had wanted to do more and be more. I was at the mercy of Jody's hands as he doled out shots and the doctor's hands as he helped me heal and then transferred small pieces of our future back to me. Noah's wife had been the same, but still showed up every day of her life. I would not yet know if this transfer would be the fulfillment of that rainbow promise by God to remember me, but for now at least the rain had stopped and the waters were calm for those embryos to enter a new land.

I know you are pacing the deck right now, searching for land and watching others get the answers to the prayers you've prayed. I know it feels like you are the stand-in for someone else's show. But one thing that I learned in this time of passivity was this: To receive God's blessing, you don't have to be the star of your universe. You just have to show up.

Guiding Questions

1. When have you felt like a spectator in your own life, along for the ride like Noah's wife?
2. How might you choose to "show up" for your life today, no matter what role you have been cast in?

Scripture

- Genesis 6:1–22, 8:1–19, 9:8–17

The Getting

Chapter 12

"The Joys of Pregnancy" and Mary Magdalene

Remember the woman who poured expensive oil on Jesus' head? The one who got all that flack for wasting what could have been put to better use? That was Mary Magdalene. She had that kind of devotion, that kind of all-consuming focus, because she had a history with Jesus. He had proven Himself to her more times than not over the years. In Luke, we see her traveling with Jesus and His disciples. She is one of the many who gave up her former life, leaving everything, including the essentials, behind because she "had been cured of evil spirits and diseases" (Luke 8:2). Jesus had cast out seven demons from her and she was better than restored; she was a new woman. She was Sigourney Weaver in *Ghostbusters* when she finally floats back to the ground, stops twitching, and begins to talk in her normal voice. No wonder Mary Magdalene wanted nothing more than to follow the man who had found and repaired her sanity; He was already her savior before He was her Savior. A bottle of oil would have seemed a small price to pay.

She was there for all the big stuff. We catch her standing below the cross, crumbling under the loss as "the earth shook and the rocks split" (Matthew 27:51) when Jesus died. We see her "sitting there opposite the tomb" (Matthew 27:61) when the guards rolled the stone in place after His body was laid to rest. We watch her return for the next three days until the Sabbath, when the next earthquake arrived and an angel descended to disrupt the still quiet dawn. And finally, because she was never too far off, we hear the good news first with her: "Do not be afraid, for I know that you are looking for Jesus who was crucified. He is not here, he has risen, just as he said" (Matthew 28:5–6).

Because of her devotion and diligence, she got to share the news. She had proven herself in the small things. She gave Him her time, which in the world as we know it, is the highest commodity. And because she had seen it all, the "joy" (Matthew 28:8) of His resurrection was hers first. She became the megaphone for the new Christian world.

Honestly, that's a lot to live up to. I read stories of the lives of women like this, and they land heavily on my chest, like trying to sift through the yellow pages without an index. I want to do it all, but I get tired at the thought. How do you really lose your life to gain it? How do you travel in the desert for forty years like Miriam or sail the seas for months like Noah's wife? How do you keep on keeping on? C. S. Lewis once wrote in *Mere Christianity* that, "[To have Faith in Christ] means, of course, trying to do all that He says . . . But trying in a new way, a less worried way." That sounds great. But how do you turn down the worry and crank up the trust?

This was where my thoughts wandered as we waited the requisite ten days after the FET before going in for the blood draw. I tried to trust and "let go and let God," but that didn't mean I didn't cheat. We were seasoned veterans, you remember. No over-the-counter twenty-dollar-a-pop pregnancy test for us. I had reviewed the numbers on the fertility bill, the multipage list with little subtraction signs next to each item. It was like winning the reverse lottery. Congratulations, you've been chosen. Deposit all your money here! Because of this, infertility had turned me into a serial saver. We clipped coupons and ate peanut butter straight from the jar and Little Caesars' Hot n' Readys without shame. So of course I had figured out where to get pregnancy tests online, in bulk, at a dollar a stick. And these puppies were sensitive. That second pink line could show up if your body was even thinking about babies. I began taking them four days after the transfer. Five days in and I had a nice, neat, if light, second pink line. I have a picture saved on my phone of eight or ten little sticks lined up on our bathroom counter with progressively darker pigments. I do not share this image with anyone because while it's a picture of our success, it is also a picture of my urine and of my obsessiveness, two things better kept to themselves. But I kept the picture, because it demarcates my way to the finish line. Despite all this, I still wasn't ready to rejoice. After all, we had been here before, just last Easter. So I would let myself release an excited breath each morning and then, with all the detachment I could muster, lay that little strip next to its fellows on the counter for Jody to inventory at his leisure, and went about my day.

Despite the super saving, I still sprung, as always, for same-day results when I went in for the official blood draw. I also got pulled over for speeding on my way to the clinic, which would have been a big negative in the bank account except for what happened next. You see, there's a shortcut to the doctor's office that is too seductive to pass up. It sings its siren song like an icy Coke on a hot day. But it also winds through an upscale neighborhood lined with houses stocked to the rafters with old money. Massive colonials and stone mansions give you the stink eye from a respectable distance. The speed limit is 30. They like you to roll in a stately manner down their avenue and take no prisoners. But on this particular day, the policeman let me go with a warning. I told him where I was headed. We had met before, he realized, upon spying a copy of a prior ticket he had issued me last spring. It was jutting out of the glove compartment, snitching. I had been on my way to the clinic that day too, to get the blood test for our last positive pregnancy test, the one that ended in miscarriage. He must have done the math on that one, because before I knew it, he was waving me on my way and wishing me luck. God bless you, sir, wherever you are.

After the blood draw, but before the results, I returned to school and once again broke the rules, carrying my phone with me the rest of the day. I rubbed it in my pocket like a totem, and when it finally vibrated, mid-lecture on run-on sentences, I startled like a rabbit and ran out of the room. This group of students was all manner of crazy, so I'm lucky no one escaped out a window during my absence. They were full of questions when I returned. I parried by giving them a free period in the last ten minutes. Works every time. Teenagers, much like the rest of us, are inherently self-serving. I could not have taught if I wanted to, because, as you might suspect, it was official. I was pregnant. I was very, very pregnant. The numbers were off the chart for this one. "Little overachiever," I remember managing to joke with the nurse over the phone.

Yet still we held our breath. It was more important that those high numbers double in the two days to follow. With our last pregnancy, forever the comparison, it had doubled in the beginning and then slowed. But despite our misgivings, the numbers continued to rise at mind-warping rates. Eventually we began to really believe that this one might stick. We wandered out of our six-week ultrasound like we'd just stepped off a rocking ship onto the dock. Having just seen one very hearty embryo with a thrumming heartbeat, like a tiny fluttering eyelash, we were still getting our land legs back. In fact, that is the best definition I can find for motherhood: an endless attempt to get your legs back.

The rest of our time at the fertility clinic was blessedly uneventful, and before we knew it, we were mapping new routes to the obstetrician's office. We had graduated. We were in the land of the fertiles. It felt very slow for a very long time, and now we were jolted by the speed.

You would expect this to be an exciting and comfortable transition, like easing into clean sheets you didn't have to put on the bed yourself. I know I certainly did. But my primary emotion was disorientation. I had not really thought about this point in the plot, so focused had I been on the events leading up to it. I was also nauseated and exhausted. And I still found it difficult to believe I was really and truly pregnant. I was spinning in circles, the dog in search of its tail. Nevertheless, we began to do the things that parents do. I downloaded an app on my phone that tracked the baby's growth in terms of varying fruits and vegetables. I had to ask my mom what an acorn squash was. We ended up Googling it. Over Christmas, my brother hauled their baby furniture out of storage and we spent the afternoon celebrating Christ's birth by assembling a monster of a crib and changing table. I have a picture of Jody with my dad and brother leaning over the edge of the white bed rail, exhausted and triumphant. We painted the only guestroom in our tiny ranch-style home a bright aqua and dubbed it the nursery. From now on, all guests could have the couch. A baby shower was in the works for late spring. I bought deceptively stretchy work pants and drank a lot of tea.

But somewhere in the midst of this, there was also a feeling of guilt. It ran like a fault line down the center of my happiness. There's always something, isn't there? I was thoroughly enjoying being a normal pregnant lady after so much tribulation, but I wasn't fall-down-on-my-knees grateful like I thought I would be. When I prayed for our future and asked God to make us a family, I imagined that once we got to this point, I would be throwing out hallelujahs like confetti. Hannah did. When she finally got pregnant with Samuel, she said, "My heart rejoices in the Lord; in the Lord my horn is lifted high. My mouth boasts over my enemies, for I delight in your deliverance" (1 Samuel 2:1). And after Jesus gave Mary Magdalene her life back from those demons, she gladly handed it back over in His service. Meanwhile, I was over here doing math. I wrung my hands over our checkbook and pictured our little family busking on street corners for change. This kid better be cute. And seriously, I could not stand Jody for one minute. My fruits of the Spirit shriveled at his approach. There was little peace, patience, or kindness. All I wanted to do when I got home from work was vomit or sleep. I felt anxiety creep in over all the new things that I was not getting right. I could not celebrate, could not adequately release the angsty vibes, and it was knitting an amazingly intricate blanket of guilt that I trailed behind me wherever I went.

I think this is the hardest awareness to grasp in a world of positive and negative, good and bad, sinners and saints. Things are not always going to be tragic or wonderful. Mary Magdalene probably grumbled on the mountainside when the sermon ran long and the rock grew hard beneath her seat. She probably snapped at the disciples when they grew sanctimonious after the ascension. You know they did. And we don't see Miriam in the thirty-fifth year in the desert or Noah's wife after six weeks of rain and the smell of damp goat. We can't leap off the page to see the bird's-eye view of the plan whenever we want, and so we are going to feel all the minutiae of the close-up.

My guilt was heavy because I expected to transcend it after every hard thing that happened to get us here. But because I watched my belly stretch and body grow into this amorphous thing that was now not wholly mine, and because students still turned in papers late, and because winter still refused to yield to spring, I got irritated, disgruntled, sad. It made me feel lost in many ways, as when the plot of the movie does not follow your best guesses and you have to remind yourself to pay attention. I hate that. I'm usually the plot-whisperer.

This was a time of joy, yes, when strangers offered me congratulations and I took the ceremonial trip to Human Resources to file for maternity leave. It was fun when Jody and I took a tour of the birthing ward at our hospital with another couple and afterward made a late-night Krispy Kreme stop because two out of four of us were pregnant. I loved the lack of appointments that normal pregnancy brought, the freedom to let the bruises from all those shots heal. But I was also skittish. I was jittery and unsure what to do in the big wide world now that we were getting what we had asked for. For me, it is often harder to be happy. It seems like more work to try and appreciate things. Hurt feels more authentic; letting the smile slide off my face became a welcome break. For me, hurt is reactionary and joy takes effort, much like marriage, motherhood, and the Christian life. I was still learning the ropes of this joy thing, and if there was one thing that I wish I had understood then that I try to practice now, it is grace, big gulps of grace.

In order to feel joy, you have to give yourself the grace to feel all the other things too. He's okay with it. He understands we each are a thousand-piece puzzle that always needs sorting.

Guiding Questions

1. When have you reacted unexpectedly to good news? Have you ever felt disoriented after finally getting what you'd hoped for?
2. Even Hannah and Miriam and Mary Magdalene weren't righteously thankful all the time. How can you extend to yourself some grace?

Scripture

- Luke 8:2
- Matthew 27:51, 27:61, 28:5–8
- 1 Samuel 2:1

Chapter 13

"The Interim" and the Widow of Zarephath

Every year during the holidays, the high school holds a hallway-decorating competition. The administration knows we all need a distraction, a fun divergence from the ever-increasing intensity of exams, to get through the final weeks. This competition is no joke. Senior girls recruit crafty moms, the ones with extra time and money who can be bribed into making multiple trips to Michael's and Hobby Lobby. Costume and prop closets in the theater department are raided and cabinets marked HALLWAY DECORATIONS in various faculty workrooms are unlocked after a year of close guarding. I think the winner gets a trophy, but that's not the point. The point is to get lost in something. It's a marvel to watch the hallways slowly transform over the course of the week . . . a skeleton of a tree held up by wires in one corner, a banquet table twelve feet long shoved against the wall, a power cord haphazardly taped across the floor. And then, after one very long final push that finds you buried in carpenter paper long past midnight, you walk in the next morning to a new world. To your left, "The Dance of the Sugar Plum Fairies" plays over a loudspeaker and glitter trails. A bigger-than-life Nutcracker stands at attention, surrounded by giant presents. Ballerinas, having been enlisted from the dance department, twirl in full costume. To your right, the entrance of a train station leads you past Platform 9 3/4 into Hogsmeade, where lights twinkle from the ceiling and volunteers in full wizard's attire (repurposed graduation robes) pass out butterbeer and hot chocolate. It is thoroughly enchanting in all the good ways.

This is how I felt leading into the holidays that Christmas. Completely distracted in all the good ways. The joy I had struggled to grasp had taken hold, momentarily. My worries had stilled when the anatomy ultrasound revealed a healthy, hearty child. And after an elaborate and epic baking day, I announced to our families via mini chocolate cupcakes filled with blue icing that we were having a boy. We even had a name. I was delighted with the world and it with me. There's something about being pregnant at Christmas when everything feels . . . more. The tacky houses lit up with purple lights got to me. The piped-in music at the mall and in elevators got to me. Even the twenty-four hours of *A Christmas Story* on television got to me. Maybe it was the hormones, but I cried like it was the last night of church camp at both the Christmas Eve service and *Charlie Brown Christmas*. Man, how do you not cry over that scraggly little tree?

So when January rolled around and classes were back in session, I somehow felt immune to the winter doldrums, like I had been inoculated against the post-holiday slump along with Tdap and MMR. As I went in for my glucose test for gestational diabetes on a dreary morning in mid-January, I was mostly thinking about lesson plans for *Pride and Prejudice* and debating what would be the least disgusting flavor of the sugar bomb they made you chug to check your insulin levels.

It was all a mistake really, what happened next.

The nurse at the front desk thought I also had an ultrasound scheduled, so after choking down the orange drink (not a winning flavor), they brought me back to the darkened room. I didn't correct them. I wasn't about to turn down a chance to peek at the little guy again. I was just beginning to feel that jumpy sugar high when they laid me on the table and warmed up the gel. By the looks of things on the screen, the baby was feeling it too. He was all over the place, a black-and-white fish in an increasingly smaller pond. When they scanned his face, he was sticking his tongue out. "Like he's daring you to catch him," I joked. I kid when I'm nervous, mouthing over my emotions. The technician nodded impassively. Sometimes you get one with the sense of humor of Bea Arthur. Actually, scratch that, Bea Arthur had a wicked sense of humor. Let's say Marlon Brando.

I had to wait an hour to let the sugar do its thing before they would send me down to the lab to have blood drawn. But instead of sending me back out with the other hyped-up moms after the ultrasound, they called me back to an exam room. My day was veering sharply off course. There was an article in *Parents* magazine lying with its page folded down in the waiting room that I had wanted to finish. Also, I needed to get back to work before lunch. The nausea from the drink was settling in, high up in my throat. I didn't want to put on a paper gown. It was cold in the room. So many thoughts skittered across my brain, it made me twitchy. I was checking my watch when my OB walked in. She had a look. It was the same look as the RE who presided over my miscarriage. This was the flight attendant face—the one meant to stem the tide of panic, despite all evidence to the contrary.

She began slowly and deliberately to explain that they were going to send me to another part of the complex, the hospital part, to see a maternal fetal medicine specialist (MFMS) for another ultrasound. They could fit me in today. A part of me, somewhere inside my mind, hardened like a peach pit. I shook my head, trying to shake the sounds out. I refused to understand. The anatomy scan had been only a few weeks before and everything was perfect. It's a boy! Remember?

She pointed to a few numbers on a tiny index card I hadn't noticed in her hand. They showed unusual abdominal and femur measurements. So, he's short. Who cares? She would not make me see something I did not want to see. But she was a juggernaut. A very nice, serious, gentle juggernaut driving home her message. She directed my attention to his tongue. Apparently, it was measuring large as well, which, with everything else combined, put him at risk for several genetic conditions. So no, not a laughing matter to see that tongue on the screen. No wonder the nurse hadn't laughed with me. She told me to call Jody and have him meet me. I said I would and then didn't. I wasn't ready to end his hard-won happiness, and also, telling him made it real. I shook my head like a woman concussed. What about the blood draw? Would I be back in time to teach the rest of my classes? She squeezed my arm and went to get me a wheelchair.

After God had sent ravens to feed the prophet Elijah, during yet another famine, He sent him to the gates of Zarephath, where he met a widow. Elijah asked, "Would you bring me a little water in a jar so I may have a drink?" (1 Kings 17:10). Easy enough. But just as she turned to fulfill the request, he tacked on an order for bread. He was like the teenager who manipulates his parents into a double feature at the movies. *If we're already here, we might as well.* But this widow was not in a position to be liberal. She told Elijah, "I don't have any bread—only a handful of flour in a jar and a little oil in a jug. I am gathering sticks to take home and make a meal for myself and my son, that we may eat it—and die" (1 Kings 17:12). You remember Naomi and Ruth and how hard it was for widows to make it on their own in biblical Israel? That's why there were so many commands to take care of the widows and orphans. This woman had no kinsman redeemer... no one to earn the literal dough. And she had a son that she had been watching slowly starve. She had no favors to grant, and she had enough fighting spirit left to point this out to Elijah.

But as prophets liked to do, Elijah pushed his point, refusing to take "no" and starvation for an answer. He told her to go home, make a small loaf from what she had, and *first* feed him and "*then* make something for yourself and your son" (1 Kings 17:13), because God was going to keep them all fed despite the evidence to the contrary.

How do you listen to that kind of request? How do you put the demands and promises of a stranger over the needs of your child? Every mother nods her head and says amen. I don't even want to share my last Tater Tot with my kids, much less a total stranger. All I can say is, God can rain down some otherworldly faith when He needs us to have it.

So the woman listened to him, and it worked, of course. The flour and oil never ran out. From little there was much, a never-ending cup.

While they wheeled me through a maze of corridors, I thought about the expectant moms still sitting in the OB's waiting room in varying stages of rotundity. I could see them, sipping water and flipping through my leftover magazine while scanning their phones. I had been there only a short time ago. And now, once again, I was on the outside—the odd woman out, on her way to another specialist for another problem. That's the thing about the unexpected complications of life. You become separate. They pick you up and put you on a shelf away from all the other toys. You are whisked out of the humming banalities of everyday life and into this new world that feels isolated. All the normal sounds of the world come at you garbled as if under water. What to eat for dinner and what's happening at work cannot matter in the same way. All you want to be able to do is scroll through Facebook and talk about Jane Austen and go to that U2 concert and gossip about a coworker, but none of it feels the same because something is pulling back the curtain to the metaphysical. You can't lose yourself in that Twitter feed because your mind is busy asking God why He can't cut you some slack and what kind of world do we live in that it has to be so hard all the time?

I felt like we had earned this baby. We had been put through our paces more than most, and much like the widow at Zarephath, we had found abundance at the end of our starvation. So what now?

After a legitimate panic attack in the MFMS office, I caved and called Jody, who answered the phone so pleasantly distracted that it broke my heart. It took me a minute to find the words that would bring him to me, sad and serious. But he came and held my hand as we had yet another ultrasound that took twice as long and accessed a much higher resolution, for greater specificity of measurements, we were informed, though we didn't ask. During the ultrasound, the technician did not speak. Neither did I. Jody continued to hold my hand and say comforting things in a whispery voice, mostly to himself. My back was so tight and legs so numb from all the lying flat that the tears that dripped down the sides of my face to wet my hair and ears were as much from pain as a reaction to our situation. I also hadn't eaten in four hours.

The doctor came in at one point after I had begged for a break to sit up and stretch and asked if we were willing to do an amniocentesis. Originally, we had decided against it. Why put our baby at unnecessary risk? But now it seemed like he already was, so we nodded and signed waivers and had it done. I didn't even feel the needle. The ultrasound confirmed a few things: the enlarged tongue and distended belly and a possible heart malformation; but it also negated others: the shorter femurs of Down and other syndromes. So our new doctor sent our amnio off to the Mayo Clinic to be analyzed for other genetic abnormalities. We would get our results in about ten days. And I had thought I was past the long waits. We were also being referred to a pediatric cardiologist to have a specialized ultrasound of the heart. For now, we could go home and "relax." It was so much information and not enough all at the same time.

It was dark when we left the hospital, walking hand in clammy hand. There were the logistics of finding two cars in opposite areas of the hospital–doctor's tower complex. I also needed to eat. We agreed to meet at a Caribbean restaurant halfway between the hospital and home. Cooking or even the effort of a sandwich was out of the question. I was aching and so hungry and stunned that I couldn't stop shaking. I drove very slowly to the restaurant. My mind was a cloud, too dense to sift through, and I leaned over the steering wheel to peer through the window as if it might show me the way.

When we finally sat down to eat, we studied the menus in silence, not yet ready to talk about what all this would mean. We ordered burgers. But when we bowed our heads to bless the meal and Jody's voice cracked, my dam broke. I cried and tore my napkin to bits and even screamed a little, I think. I imagine it put a few patrons off their dinner. I didn't care. The burgers were cold by the time we got around to eating. In the end, the only thing that kept us going was the uncertainty. We did not really know what any of this would mean. It could all be nothing, and this could be the scare that we would speak of with voices hushed by gratefulness, the thing I would whisper over my sleeping son. Or this could be everything. Even the experts weren't sure. We would have to wait for more information. Finally, we settled our bill and went home, because we both had work the next day. Time marches on.

The Bible does not say how long Elijah and the widow and her son enjoyed their bottomless bowls. All we know is that "some time later" the woman's son becomes so sick that "he grew worse and worse, and finally stopped breathing" (1 Kings 17:17). From empty to full to empty again like Naomi. This widow reacts as I would have predicted based on her first encounter with Elijah. She points a finger at him, saying,

"What do you have against me, man of God? Did you come to remind me of my sin and kill my son?" (1 Kings 17:18). He had made a miracle happen in her small household. But just as she settled into normalcy, sickness struck. She had witnessed the power of God. But she did not yet know if He was good. We do not know how many prayers she issued before her son took that last final breath, but we do catch the fallout. Anger and guilt. Anger at Elijah and God for letting her son die and guilt over her own sin, whatever list of vices she had running in her head at the time, the tally that all mothers keep.

That's always the question, isn't it? That nagging wondering thought in the back of your mind over whether God really has our best interests at heart, because if He doesn't, then don't we have to earn the goodness? Any sin could result in the flip of the scales and the end of prosperity. Because this is all we see. We live in a world where faults are punished and good deeds rewarded. Run a red light, get a ticket. But sometimes it gets murky, right? Maybe you see someone run the light and they get away with it. Or no one thanks you for the donation to the church's backpack drive. We comfort ourselves with the idea that it all balances out in the end. Karma and the yin and the yang of it. We are always keeping a ledger, so it seems impossible that God isn't keeping one too. The widow saw good rewarded: Feed the prophet, feed yourselves. And she saw the bad punished: Sin and your son dies. It's hard to step away from that. But Elijah prayed for the boy and God healed him. The woman saw good come around again. I always thought this story was about the goodness God shows you when you have faith. But that's not really it. It's about God showing goodness in spite of us.

As Jody and I sat there over our cold food while the restaurant emptied of customers, we did not yet know how our story would play out and what the future would look like for us or for our son, who was safe for now, still tucked inside. I was more like that widow than not. I was unsure all over again if God really cared, and lining up my wrongs to see which one had tipped the scale. The magic of Christmas and the distractions of everyday life had been cast aside by one accidental ultrasound. I was thrown back into a sea of doubt.

It's easy to let your own tally of rights and wrongs and vices and virtues paint your picture of God. But God is not so tied to your timeline. He sees the beginning, middle, and forever of you, and will work events toward His glory and your future as His child. You can take refuge in that.

Guiding Questions

1. When has your life veered sharply off course?
2. How, like the widow of Zarephath, could you help someone else today despite your situation?
3. Have you ever viewed God as a judge measuring your sins and good deeds like checks and balances? When has He shown you goodness despite your deeds?

Scripture

- 1 Kings 17:7–23

Chapter 14

"The Uncertainty" and Martha

There were a great deal of Marys in the Bible. They were the "Catherines" and "Jennifers" of the eighties and the "Madelines" and "Kelseys" of the nineties. We've got the biggie—Mary, the mother of Jesus—and we've got Mary Magdalene, who, along with a few other women, traveled with Jesus and the disciples, and then we've got Mary, Martha's sister. This is the Mary who makes me laugh. She is so very much the younger child.

Jesus came to a small village where He decided to stay in the home of the sisters, Martha and Mary. Martha hosted a dinner, and because Jesus moved with an entourage, there was a lot of work to do. Think Thanksgiving-watt work. This was week-long prepping and basting and kneading and cleaning and all the other hundreds of things that are the reasons why I am never asked to host. It's a work of art, a Sherlock Holmes puzzle cracked, if you can make everything move like the innards of a clock. Now I want you to picture your husband on Thanksgiving. And I want you to imagine him forgetting the ice—the *one* thing you asked him to do. Whatever you are feeling right now, I want you to direct toward Mary, because this is essentially what she did. She was the cog in the works.

Instead of helping Martha with the meal, Mary "sat at the Lord's feet listening to what he said" (Luke 10:39). And Martha, frazzled and "distracted by all the preparations that had to be made" (Luke 10:40), lost her cool and complained to Jesus. She tattled. Can't you just picture her: throwing a grimy kitchen towel over her shoulder, blowing a strand of hair out of her eyes, and saying, "Lord, don't you care that my sister has left me to do the work by myself? Tell her to help me!" (Luke 10:40).

When we finally lay down to sleep on that freezing January night, exhausted from a day populated with concerned doctors wielding needles and grainy images, we knew it was just the beginning. We knew the results from the amniocentesis could take up to two weeks to return. We knew we still had to face whatever images the cardiologist uncovered on yet another screen. We knew that the right people were doing what needed to be done and all that was left was for us to hold hands in the dark and pray and wait. At first this was comforting. Like a child who sits outside the office, nervous but with a little relief, while his parents and teachers discuss the bullying he's endured. What is an insurmountable problem for a seven-year-old must surely be solvable by the grown-ups. Right?

But I'm the kid who can't sit still. I'm the one inching closer to the door trying to figure out the plan. My helplessness took a turn. Less than a week into our wait, I began to get the itch—the itch to know something, do something, anything to alleviate the pressure. I called the cardiologist's nurse over and over, checking for cancellations to see if she could get us in any sooner. I called both our OB and our new MFMS to discuss the ultrasound images again. I questioned why none of this had been found on the anatomy scan. Isn't that what it's for? Forget the pink or blue cupcakes. The point was to make sure that everything was as it should be. I caught myself hugging my stomach, like I could somehow protect my son from all that waited in the outside world. It was a terrible state to live in, and I did not live it well.

For better or worse, I am totally a Martha. We always went skiing or hiking for family vacations. I was raised on the refrain of "let's pick up the pace." Once, I was left, a little kid in a fuchsia snowsuit, alone on a mountain. It was an accident. I walked back to the hotel, clunking along in unforgiving boots. I have walked with large strides ever since, chasing the ghost of a speeding adult or chasing my own shadow. It took me years to discover and begin to appreciate the deliciousness of lying on the beach with nothing but a cold drink and a good book. It was so decadent and goal-less. I had to acclimatize. I remember the first time my husband announced that he was going to take a nap on a Sunday afternoon. I thought only children napped.

This drive for activity is not inherently bad. It made me a good teacher and a lifelong learner, naturally curious about the workings of people and various pursuits. One slow summer home from college, I bought a cello on eBay. I thought I could teach myself. Nope. But it looked nice in the corner, next to the unfinished copy of *Anna Karenina*. What a weird summer. I briefly ran a cupcake business, which my friends and family still recall and often request. And during graduate school, all available floor space of my first tiny duplex was taken up by an easel and paint supplies. I thought I might be an artist and didn't know it yet. It was terrible and messy and lovely and therapeutic, kind of like running in the rain. As innate as doing and seeking are for me, resting and trusting are hard-won. It always feels like a trick. Why did you give me this gift card for a massage? Do you think I'm too tense? Why read chick lit when you can read Faulkner? Spa treatments and beaches and naps were for other people with less to accomplish. The ego rings loud here.

So Martha, the "doer," complained, probably to draw attention to how hard she was working. She wanted a thank-you. But Jesus rarely does what we want. He chooses instead to give us what we need. He said to the fretting Martha, "You are worried and upset about many things, but only one thing is needed. Mary has chosen what is better, and it will not be taken away from her" (Luke 10:41–42). Mary got it right, annoying as it is. She chose to sit and listen to the words of her teacher instead of checking things off the list. She made it about Him and not her. She gave her time, which is the hardest thing to sacrifice. Martha saw her agenda as more important because she was getting things done. Yes, that meal needed fixing and those places needed setting, but she couldn't trust Jesus enough to stop to take a breather. She was chasing her shadow.

I could not let go of the need to control, and the wait began to make me crazy. But in the end, there was literally nothing I could do to speed things up or change the outcome. Much like the conception process, this was a problem too big for me. And right in the middle of all my efforts, Jesus found a way to force me to acknowledge my own inadequacy, to put down the sieve that I was so busy trying to fill with sand. It was the call from the MFMS with the amnio analysis. The results were inconclusive. The chromosomal defect did not fit any of the major syndromes. But there were definitely chromosomal alternations. They were sending the amnio back to the Mayo Clinic for further testing.

I tried to rally. I stood in the empty conference room at work and began to fire off questions. So when should we expect the new results? She didn't know. It could take a month, or longer, or less. Had they narrowed it down to a few specific disorders? She could not say at this time. Was there more testing we could do on my end while we waited? No, not at this time. Locked doors at every turn. I hung up the phone with less of a handle on my situation than before. It wasn't the end of the long wait. It was the beginning, all over again, with no end in sight. I was stunned into submission, like a deer in the road, and like Martha. What else could I do but stop and pray? And so I did. For about thirty seconds, until I began pacing circles around the conference table like a tiger in a cage. With nothing else to do, I walked and muttered and rolled my shoulders and tried to accept my place at this impasse.

There's a scene in John that Luke does not include in his account of the sisters. It describes an earlier visit by Jesus. It is a story with which I am sure you are familiar. The sisters had a brother, Lazarus, who was dying. They sent for Jesus to come to Bethany so that He could save their brother. They had faith, after all, that He was the great healer. He got word and said, "This sickness will not end in death. No, it is for God's glory so that God's Son may be glorified through it" (John 11:4). Thank goodness, the grown-up had a plan. But two days passed as they looked to the horizon. And Lazarus died. And the sisters wept and mourned and placed him in the tomb. When Jesus finally arrived, they came out to greet Him with tears and admonishments. Martha said, "If you had been here, my brother would not have died" (John 11:21). Because of Lazarus' death and how close their little town was to the metropolis of Jerusalem, many people had come to grieve with the sisters. They followed Jesus to the tomb like curious, sad groupies. And thus, many were there to see what happened next. Jesus yelled, "Lazarus, come out!" (John 11:43) and the dead man walked forward, shaking off the funky-smelling burial rags. The events worked precisely in the order and manner Jesus had planned to bring the greatest honor to God. There *was* a plan. Martha just didn't get to hatch it.

Even if conception had been easy for Jody and me, if fertility treatments had gone like clockwork, if pregnancy had proceeded unhindered or unmarred, I would still have had these same expectations to break, these same thorns in my squishy side. I am a Martha trying to be a Mary.

We all bring what we have to the table, and God uses it to make the meal. We are not always the daughters, wives, sisters, mothers we want to be. We are a bundle of knots that God is gently untangling. But He will always use your circumstances for good. Sitting still, giving thanks, giving in to the idea that you are not steering the ship takes practice. But nothing can describe the moment when the knot finally comes free.

Guiding Questions

1. Are you a Martha or a Mary?
2. Have you ever found yourself with nothing to do but wait for God? How do you practice trust during the wait?
3. What's the knot you know needs loosening the most?

Scripture

- Luke 10:38–42

Chapter 15

"The Resting" and Mary, the Betrothed

It was a gorgeous late winter day. The sky was the kind of blue that promised spring. The trees had tiny buds, and the forsythia had already made a good showing. It was a Wednesday, but I was not in school because there was no school today. We were playing in the district basketball semifinals at noon. The high school declared it an impromptu holiday. This is what happens when you've got snow days to kill. What's better than a repurposed snow day? Nothing. The joy and energy of it are incomparable, and teenagers at school sporting events are a thing to behold. They are like toddlers at Halloween. Everyone is hyped up on school spirit and sugar and adrenaline, even me.

We tailgated and then, as I drove to watch some boys run around on a court, I rolled down the windows because I actually felt sixteen again. Enormously pregnant and sixteen. But still. Just last week we had survived the visit to the cardiologist, which turned out better than we had hoped. Originally, they had thought our son had a congenital heart defect called "transposition of the great arteries," which basically means the arteries are twisted and shooting blood to all the wrong places, like a misdirected pneumatic tube at the ATM. This meant that the heart would have to work twice as hard to give the body all the oxygen it needs. Typically, these babies need surgery right after birth. There is nothing like the idea of open-heart surgery on a one-day-old to send you to your knees in prayer. I kept picturing frogs on a dissection table, which sent me into hysterics. But when the cardiologist looked closer, he gave us the all-clear, all things pumping accordingly. We were so happy leaving his office, we stumbled and laughed all the way to the car. I was still high enough off the news to sing loudly in my car to Alan Jackson and honk my horn with the rest of the caravan. Only really good or really bad news makes me turn to country music. I had even let a few cheerleaders write all over my car with what they swore was washable paint. CLASS OF 2012 and SENIOR STATE CHAMPS slanted down the back windows in glitter and gold. It was Christmas hallway decorating all over again. I was happy to be alive and feeling the spirit of the season.

Wearing Mardi Gras beads and an electric purple polyester T-shirt that stretched over my belly, I shuffled into the gym. Taking a seat with a few other teachers, I propped my feet up on the seat in front of me, my legs aching from the traverse up the stadium steps. It was a great game. We ate smuggled-in trail mix and licorice ropes, and the college counselor sitting next to me whisper-yelled a few minutes into the second quarter that she was pregnant. I laughed and welcomed her into the club. We yelled, "Go Big Gold!" and did the wave. And the worry of the last weeks was not with me for a moment.

We won, of course, and I fist-bumped with the best of them while walking back to my car, reminding a few that they did, in fact, have "real school" tomorrow. Yeah, I was *that* teacher. Peeling off my beads and pulling on a sweatshirt, I tamped the vibes a little and headed to an ultrasound with my OB. Because I was now considered high risk, I had to have them every week. I spent most of the drive trying to calculate what day we might get off next week for the state championship. The afternoon light and the recent win carried me there.

The technicians had stopped speaking to me. They must have put something in my chart: "Warning, highly sensitive material, do not break seal." When I went back to an exam room for the post-ultrasound rundown with my doctor, I barely had time to sit before a nurse popped in with a gown. I wasn't scheduled to have an exam, and I let her know it. I was done with surprises. And I was not about to have a physical if I could help it, like sticking a Q-tip into an infected eardrum just for kicks. The nurse, looking at a spot above my head, repeated the doctor's orders and ducked out. I had the exam.

After a few tortuous and awkward minutes, the doctor pulled her gloves off, told me to sit up, and said, "Okay, nothing too serious here, but your ultrasound showed a higher level of amniotic fluid and your cervix feels a little ripe, so I'm going to send you home on bed rest."

I blinked a few times. I crossed my legs and smoothed the paper under my thighs. I was buying time. Meanwhile, the ticker tape in my head read: *What do you mean, ripe? I just stuck my toe in the third trimester. You better take another look, sister, because this mama is not yours for the picking.* I said none of this, of course. And silence fell, like a wet blanket. She picked it up and continued on. "This happens all the time," she assured me. "Your body just needs rest. Stay off your feet. Let someone else take care of you for a change."

For a change? Who were we kidding? That's all I'd done for the past two years. I squeezed my knees tighter. "By 'off my feet,' you mean sit, right?"

" 'Off your feet' means off the floor," she clarified. "Keep them elevated and remain in a reclining position. We are trying to remove the pressure of gravity here," she explained.

Oh good. All we have to do is beat Newton's Third Law.

It would be tragic to write a book on motherhood and not discuss Mary, Jesus' mom, the motherlode of mothers. Talk about the opposite of infertile. She was a virginal wellspring of life. Mary was a woman (girl really) with her future set out before her like a nice set of china. She had a fiancé. She was in her prime. And she must have had a pretty good head on her shoulders to have already "found favor with God" (Luke 1:30). Most teenagers and adults flit in and out like birds at a feeder. But what I really like about her is that when the angel of the Lord appeared to her and said, with a duly noted exclamation point: "Greetings, you who are highly favored! The Lord is with you" (Luke 1:28), she did not immediately rejoice. Instead, she was "greatly troubled at his words and wondered what kind of greeting this might be" (Luke 1:29). And for good reason. The Lord never asks the easy or predictable of us. How does one digest the fact that you're about to gestate a boy who will be "great and will be called the Son of the Most High . . . and he will reign over the house of Jacob forever" (Luke 1:32, 33)? She needed clarification. But he just passed her his card and gave a referral, her cousin: Elizabeth, the formerly barren one now pregnant with John. So there was nothing left to do but accept, through a serious dose of supernatural trust, that all would proceed accordingly. This girl of a woman must have taken a mighty breath before saying, "I am the Lord's servant . . . May it be as you have said" (Luke 1:38). Whenever I pray that, it comes out snarky.

I thought I was taking my doctor's orders in stride, as best I could, while walking to the nurses' desk to check out. I hadn't had to duck my head and Lamaze breathe once. But as I was in the middle of negotiating my next appointment for anytime after three so I wouldn't have to miss work, my doctor put a gentle and unmoving hand on my shoulder. And then she said, "Bed rest means no work."

I made it as far as the car. And then I lost it. I cried big snotty tears and kicked the tires, like it was the car's fault. What was I supposed to do? I needed a substitute. But a sub couldn't teach the rest of my *1984* unit. Everybody knew they were only good for crowd control. I was supposed to collect those essays tomorrow. Who would remind that one kid that it was due sixth period so he would finish it in study hall instead of nap? Who would take the dog out before Jody got home? Who was going to pull the trash cans to the curb on Sunday night before the garbage truck came early Monday morning? Jody never remembered.

I called him sobbing about trash while sitting in my car outside the Chinese restaurant, where I was getting take-out because, apparently, I wouldn't be cooking anytime in the near future. Motherhood is often like this, a continually changing plan that has you kicking the tires and eating fried rice.

It's hard to suddenly be thrown out of the current that has

been moving you so efficiently toward your goals. But I had no choice. I did not teach the next day or the next. I withdrew myself to the couch, where I languished, like a Victorian. I watched the rain wash the "2012" off the windows of my car as it sat unused in the drive. Someone else collected my essays and brought them to my house later in the week. If I'd had my way, I would have begun grading them the day they were due. Everyone knows the rate of teenage interest in making corrections is directly proportionate to how quickly they are returned. Also, essay grading was an excellent distraction. But my life was at a standstill. Jody was at work and the hours dragged. Once my lesson plans were complete and turned in for the sub (*that ineffectual second-stringer*, I thought wryly), I had nothing to do. Except notice all the things I wanted to do. The walls in here needed a paint job. And we still hadn't put the stroller together. It was sitting in a box on the floor in the kitchen. There was dust collecting on the glass TV stand. We needed a bumper for the glass TV stand. What were we thinking owning something so absolutely not kid-friendly as a glass TV stand?

Joseph was probably a pretty decent guy. Both Mary and God saw something in him that was worth a second look. But he was still human. Which is why he planned to "divorce her quietly" so as not to "expose her to public disgrace" when he found out she was pregnant (Matthew 1:19). The Bible does not say how much time passed after Mary found out about her impending pregnancy before Joseph did. We don't know if she told him in person or he got wind of it through relatives. It was a small town after all. If I were Mary, I would have waited as long as possible. I'm a sucker for the long pause. Maybe he heard the news and stalked off. Maybe he sat stunned. Either way, he eventually came to the conclusion that it would be better for them to go through with the wedding and then deal with it later. It was both kind and practical. But God does not always want the practical. "Joseph, son of David," the angel said, "do not be afraid to take Mary home as your wife, because what is conceived in her is from the Holy Spirit" (Matthew 1:20). I hear "Holy Spirit" in Steve Martin's revival voice.

Imagine Mary. She's probably begun to show. Rumors are flying. She went from the girl with the respectable plan to the girl with an unbelievable excuse for an unwed pregnancy. She knew the truth. Do you think she ever missed getting lost in the wedding planning or gossiping at the well? Do you think she wished just for a moment that she could click her heels and be normal again?

This quiet period, while Joseph sorted out his feelings and life turned a new course, was perhaps the loneliest time in young Mary's life. But the solitude was part of the maturing process. It would turn her into the Mary who could one day sing, "My soul glorifies the Lord and my spirit rejoices in God my savior . . . From now on all generations will call me blessed, for the Mighty One has done great things for me—holy is his name" (Luke 1:47–49). The lifeguards call rest periods for a reason. It's so you can sit a minute or five and gather your strength. Treading water is hard work.

Because my OB had been so nonchalant in her concern for the baby when she ordered bed rest, it felt more precautionary than anything. I actually drafted a plea to the principal to move a couch from the student lounge into my classroom so that I could teach lying down, Cleopatra-style. If I had to be still, I wanted my mind to move. The truth is that I was terrified of the still-anticipated amnio results. I was terrified of labor. And deeper still, I was terrified of the kind of mother I would be. Teaching I could do. But mothering was foreign territory.

When you lose the thing you're hiding behind (job, children, youth, spouse), you face the fears normally blurred by the busyness of life. They come into sharp focus and you must sit with them, commune with them, and let God show you how He will carry you through each one. They are not as scary if you remember you're not facing them alone.

Guiding Questions

1. When have you found yourself taken out of the current of your life by unexpected events? How did you handle it? How could you handle it differently now?

2. What fears or worries do you think will show up if you slow down? How can you find the peace to overcome them?

3. Does Mary's response to her unplanned pregnancy offer you strength to face your own unexpected turns in the road?

Scripture

- Luke 1:26–28, 1:47–49
- Matthew 1:18–25

Chapter 16

"The Fruition" and Mary's L&D

Road trips are hard when you're pregnant. Road trips are hard in general for someone like me who, first, has the bladder of an eighty-year-old. I know now to limit my liquid intake two hours before departure. Also, as mentioned ad nauseum, my feet tended to swell with the force of gravity. Both sitting and standing were equally debilitating. After a while I looked like Gumby, legs gently widening until they met ground, like bell-bottoms. The medical term for this is *pregnancy-induced edema*. If you pushed a finger into my calf, the imprint would linger, as in those collectible oily stickers from the nineties or Play-Doh. Second, I have a bad back. I've had it all my life. Genetic thanks go out to my mom on this one. She still has a poem I wrote for her in elementary school entitled "Back's Out No Doubt." It involved lots of cheery suggestions like Häagen-Dazs and heating pads. The first time my back went out was in college while painting my grandmother's living room. The upward motion of the roller did me in, and I spent the twelve-hour ride home flat on the backseat. During pregnancy, car rides longer than half an hour left a dull pain at the base of my spine, which dug a little deeper with every mile, like someone taking you hostage with a butter knife. And finally, third trimester nausea is no joke. I needed carsickness bags to get down the block.

For all of the reasons mentioned above, I cannot begin to imagine what it was like for Mary on a donkey traveling from Nazareth to Bethlehem. That's about seventy miles. How fast does a donkey walk? Not fast enough. It doesn't seem like a smooth ride either. Also, there's a thing all throughout pregnancy that only intensifies toward the end: extreme thirst. Your blood volume increases to feed the placenta and everything else, and that takes a lot of liquid—you are a sponge that cannot get full. I can't imagine how Mary must have felt, except when I picture that scene from *Three Amigos* where Martin Short and Steve Martin shake the last drops from their canteens in the middle of the desert, while Chevy Chase rinses and spits and applies lip balm. But Mary and Joseph had no choice except to head toward Bethlehem because of the Roman census. This wasn't a babymoon. This was a government decree. So they went and no wonder we read shortly thereafter, "The time came for the baby to be born" (Luke 2:6). Road trips will do that to you.

Bed rest for me was one long road trip. I was stuck watching the world go by my window. I was waiting to get to my destination. But I had respected my doctor's orders, ever the rule follower, and stayed off my feet for the better part of a week. I'd graded essays and read books and watched the first season of *Downton Abbey*. How had I been so out of the loop? That house! Those clothes! Maggie Smith! My OB had called me that Monday to check in, and other than the seriously annoying back pain and edema despite keeping my feet up, I was okay. No contractions. Nothing. If all went well with my ultrasound on Thursday, we could discuss my return to work. Freedom was in sight.

So when the high school made it to the state championship on Wednesday, I was in the mood to celebrate. Jody came home to keep me company and watch the game and even picked up gyros and fries from our favorite Greek place. It was raining again and the back pain was distractingly uncomfortable, but I was momentarily stayed by the food and company.

Not long into the first quarter, we got a call from the generic number that could mean OB, MFMS, or any other medical professional within a half mile of the hospital complex. I almost didn't answer. I wasn't in the mood. I just wanted to enjoy my meal and the game and not think for an hour or two. But you don't ignore that number. It was our MFMS. She had finally gotten the results back from the Mayo Clinic. I put her on speaker phone. We had a diagnosis. I don't remember watching the rest of the game or finishing my fries or how the afternoon passed. But I remember the first time I had to ask our doctor how to spell *Beckwith-Wiedemann syndrome*.

BWS, we would come to find out, is an overgrowth syndrome, meaning our son would be larger than most kids his age until around age eight, when his growth would start to slow. This was why he always measured weeks ahead in size on ultrasounds. Apparently, his adult-size self would be normal. Some kids, in the early years, show uneven growth where one side is larger than the other. Other potential side effects could include an enlarged tongue, which we had already seen, an opening in the abdomen wall, creases in the ears, kidney abnormalities, and abnormally large organs. And children with BWS are at a greater risk for certain types of cancers in the kidneys and liver. Our son would have to have blood draws every six weeks until age four and abdominal ultrasounds every twelve weeks until age eight to monitor for these cancers. We would be contacted by a geneticist as well as a bunch of other "-ists," who would follow his condition.

This was a lot to take in on a Wednesday afternoon in March when my biggest concern just moments earlier had been that I needed more ketchup.

The MFMS assured us that it was great news to find this out in utero so that we could be prepared before delivery. She also said it was impossible to know which of the potential characteristics he might have. We also didn't know to what degree he would be affected. Was the tongue only mildly enlarged so that he might have a tendency to leave his mouth open, or was it severely enlarged to the point of hindering breathing and eating and speaking? We would no longer be having our baby at the fancy hospital where we took that tour so long ago, but instead at the teaching hospital attached to the children's hospital, where all the experts lived.

With the basketball game on mute, Jody and I tried to talk about it. We tried to reassure ourselves that the medical experts would know what to do when the time came and that, maybe, hope upon hope, it might not be that bad. We prayed for our little guy, still safe and sound inside his sleeping bag. We placed hands on my stomach and whispered for him to sit tight, be brave, we loved him. And then later that evening I ate some Oreos and milk and Jody left to play hockey. It wasn't that we were okay. It's that we didn't know what to do. Nothing was in our hands at the moment, and talking through the various outcomes was getting exhausting, like the climactic scene in *War Games* when Matthew Broderick finally teaches the computer to give up an unwinnable game of tic-tac-toe. Sometimes nobody wins.

Jody's hockey game was late, 10 p.m. or so, and he had spent the last two hours debating whether he should even go. He had just found out some seriously heavy news, and his wife was on bed rest and whimpering occasionally like a cornered animal. But in the end, I had him bring me the heating pad and shooed him out the door. I knew the game would be a stress reliever, and I needed him to be the calm, centered one so I could freak out at my leisure. He made it off the exit ramp near the sports complex before turning around. Later, he would say he just couldn't shake the feeling that something was wrong.

When he got home, he found me lying curled up on the bed, crying, in much the same state that he had found me upon returning from the U2 concert. Clearly, he should never leave the house. I just could not get comfortable. The minute I thought I'd found a position with some relief, my back seized up all over again. We Googled "contractions" to see if that was this, but nothing we read fit my symptoms. I was only thirty weeks. We hadn't even gotten to the delivery part of the "pregnancy through birth" DVD I had borrowed from the science department. It was still sitting on that dangerous glass TV stand. In the end, we decided to phone the doctor on call. She didn't seem too concerned. She told me it sounded like possible dehydration (remember that weighty placenta), and ordered me to drink some water and see. I chugged as much as

The Getting

I could and went to bed with a sloshing stomach. But a glass of water was not going to fix this. In the end, because of the level of pain I was in and the lack of sleep we were getting, we decided to come into triage and get checked out. We remembered to go to the teaching hospital . . . just in case. I was ready to go. Home was becoming claustrophobic. Give me the steroid shots to unclench my back and I will happily hang out in your ER all night.

The night had just rolled over from Wednesday to Thursday and there was no one on the highway as we drove to this different hospital, the parking garage a different maze we had yet to solve. I joked, as we pulled up crookedly to the curb, that maybe they could do a drive-thru shot and have me back in my own bed before sunup. Remember, I'm a jokester when I'm nervous.

By the time we dragged ourselves into the ER admitting area, no one was laughing. I was guzzling water and spewing abuse at Jody, myself, and anyone else who looked askance. The discomfort had me flailing and leaning and groaning in all directions. This pain was many-fingered. Finally, as Jody signed our life away at the front desk, I retreated to the restroom to scream in peace. Side note: Do not ever visit this restroom. It's a petri dish of unidentified substances.

Finally, after I had lived a hundred lives in one, two nurses rolled me to a tiny curtained area. It offered only a suggestion of privacy. I didn't care. You could have stripped me down in the waiting area if it meant drugs at the end. They hooked probes to my belly that gave a readout like a seismograph. They were going to find out where I was on the Richter scale. They asked the standard question when a pregnant woman walks into the ER: How long have you been contracting? I kept trying to convince them, to make them see, that I wasn't contracting. It was just my back. I was not in labor. Liar, the needles screamed. I was contracting in full force. Never trust Google with your symptoms. I begged for whatever drugs they used to stop labor. Stop this train. I want off. But when the nurse gave me the physical exam, I was six centimeters dilated. The brakes gave out.

Mary did not have the option to phone ahead to let Bethlehem Memorial know they were coming. She went into labor without a place to sleep and without a doctor or sterile environment. She did it, though. She had that baby in a barn with the animals, which probably looked a lot like the ER bathroom. I'm sure she was terrified. This was not the plan. If He was the son of God, she probably assumed the real father would provide a nice place for Him to spend His first night as a human. But life doesn't go the way we anticipate. Baby Jesus did, however, get a serenade. It was the best lullaby in the history of the world with a host of angels singing, "Glory to God in the highest" and donkeys braying and shepherds praying (Luke 2:14–15).

By the end of it all, my "host" consisted of my OB, who had come in despite not being on call (a miracle of its own in the medical profession), two nurses, the anesthesiologist, and ten or so other specialists and residents-in-training. We got the big room. Because the confirmation of our son's diagnosis had arrived just hours prior, they knew who to have at the ready, a blessing we recognized despite the chaos. Before they all arrived, though, the scene was more intimate with just one nurse hooking me up to a few machines. It would have been a sweet stolen moment if it weren't for the fact that Jody and I just looked at each other, stunned, with mouths gaping like dolts. Weren't we here to get a shot for my back? Forty-five minutes later, I was fully dilated. It was time to push. This would be my first all-nighter. The first of many, as it would turn out.

There are some things you can't prepare for. One of those things is the sight of your own uterus in a mirror. "The mirror is here to help motivate you during the pushing," the nurse chirped, when I tried to kick it away with my foot. She must have been no more than twenty. She had also brought out a blue hat and blanket for "Mom to dress the baby" afterward. Someone had not given her the lowdown. We would not be cuddling our thirty-week BWS baby after delivery. We'd be lucky to get a glimpse before he was whisked off to the NICU, and that was if all went well. My mouth went dry. I looked away while my doctor grabbed the blanket and tossed it out the door with the nurse. I never saw her again. I hope she grew her wings and became a full-fledged nursling. Meanwhile, Jody was adrift. He didn't know what to do with his hands, with his words, with his eyes. He just avoided the mirror and held on to me and the bedrail for dear life. I don't think he knew we were having a baby until the whole thing was over and done.

But after cold sweats and nausea, there was an odd relief of transferring pain from one place, my back, to another, my uterus. I was doing this, ready or not. And after less than an hour of pushing, we had our son. I heard him cry loud and short and they let me kiss his slimy head, a moment so full I cannot describe and so will not try. And then they took him

away. The ten people in the background surged to the fore-
front and became twenty and the little clear box that had been
sitting in the corner unnoticed came to life with lights and a
humming and sucking sound. Try as I might, I couldn't even
see the tips of a toe. All was white light and a pulsing behind
my eyes.

I kept begging Jody to tell me what was going on. Alarms
rang out over and over. Suddenly, the alarms were closer, all
around me, and the doctor ordered Jody to focus on me now,
because I was turning a greenish gray and the world was tilt-
ing weirdly. I was icy cold and someone yelled for anesthesia.
A glimpse in the mirror showed something from the *Walking
Dead*. Total carnage. I lay back and closed my eyes. A tremen-
dous sound of liquid splashed across the floor like someone
tossing out a bucket of dirty mop water. This was followed by
a slow drip like a leaky faucet. And then I was calm, so calm I
fell asleep. Later, Jody would tell me that I had hemorrhaged,
passed out, and was on the verge of being rushed to the operating room. It was only through the efforts of my doctor, her
eyes closed in concentration and working only by feel, that
the bleeding stopped. She had to toss her tennis shoes after
leaving bloody footprints down the hall. We are women, hear
us roar.

Meanwhile, our son had been rolled away in the incubator
and we were not told when we would see him. The lack of
information was maddening, and I was not in a position to
fight it as I swung in and out of consciousness. I didn't know
how much he weighed or what color his hair was or whether
he was breathing on his own or not. We were left in that
delivery room, suddenly cavernous without all the nurses and

doctors in swatches of blue. Jody was instructed not to move while they cleaned up the bloody floor. Less than six hours had passed since we left our house. My ultrasound appointment to see if I could go back to work was in three hours.

I don't know whether Mary processed the significance of the timeline she had just crossed in her postnatal haze or if it took days, months, or years, but she did take a moment and "treasured up all these things and pondered them in her heart" (Luke 2:19). She remembered to remember, whether she could make sense of it just then or not. And that is what I did in those moments of stillness without a child in me or a doctor near me. I memorized it all. It would take me a long while before I could ponder any of what had occurred, or what would occur later, but God knew to keep it sharp in my mind. The outlines of His grace appeared later like negatives on film. There was a reason I was home on bed rest and already had the entire high school faculty praying for me. There was a reason we had received the diagnosis that very day. There was a reason Jody turned the car around and did not play hockey. There was a reason we drove to this hospital and not the other. There was a reason my OB forsook sleep to come in on her night off. There was a reason. I didn't see any of that in the moment, but I see it now. I see the tangled mess that turned into a safety net which brought our son, Charlie, into this world. And I see what Mary meant when she sang, "He has been mindful of the humble state of his servant ... For the Mighty One has done great things for me" (Luke 1:48–49).

None of us can predict all the turnings of life. I know some things have not turned out as you pictured. And I know it hurts to be in the chaos and the exhaustion of a life lived moment to moment. But even the smallest things have already been thought through by someone greater than you and me. God has a plan He's already stitched together for you, and it is masterful and, lucky for all of us, already complete.

Guiding Questions

1. When has hindsight shown you God's orchestration behind events?
2. How might you, like Mary, ponder these things, and find gratitude and joy in your journey?

Scripture

- Luke 2:1–21, 1:48–49, 2:19

The Appreciating

Chapter 17

"The Village" and Mary with Teenage Jesus

The position of motherhood is an odd one. Good job, you grew this new being in you and pushed it out. Now go take care of it. You should be an expert. Almost anyone can grow a tomato, but that doesn't mean I know what fertilizer to use or how to keep the rabbits away. It's the same principle as infertility. You are expected to be able to conceive a child "naturally." But nature doesn't always work in our favor. Some things that come "naturally" to others will not for you. Nature is not always on our side. Show me the woman who's a natural at breastfeeding and I'll try not to push her gently off my moving sidewalk.

There's this implicit belief in the "mothering instinct" or the "mom gene." Don't know if he's crying because he's hungry or tired? Just listen to your gut and you'll know what to do. Think colic shouldn't last for four hours? Don't worry. You'll figure it out once your mom reflex kicks in. Lies. Lies. Lies. I'm calling it, people. New mothers need all the help they can get. The only instincts I had when I became a mother were panic and confusion—the same emotions I had while trying to get pregnant. This was a brave new world, but I was still the same me.

And once again, like infertility, my world was not most people's. The Neonatal Intensive Care Unit is an odd place. The hospital where I delivered Charlie connected to the children's hospital that housed the NICU through a labyrinth of hallways and elevators and oddly painted floors designed to make the journey easier. Follow the red stars to the blue circles to the green squares and then take the orange elevators to the sixth floor. And after that you'll find a rabbit to lead you the rest of the way. You had to *really* want it. To gain admittance to the NICU, we signed in at the front desk and waved our wristbands. We were allowed to name four other people who could visit without us present. Their names went on a VIP list. We didn't even know what day it was that first time they asked us to choose our favorites, but we figured you couldn't go wrong with grandparents. Is there such a thing as the grandparent instinct? I bet so.

Once given the green light, you walked past a white board that showed how many babies were currently in residence, anywhere from seventy to over one hundred, given the phase of the moon. I would later learn that the higher number meant Charlie had been moved around to make space, and it would take an extra ten minutes to find him. It's 11 a.m., do you know where your children are? Beyond the white board were various hallways with lettered pods (clusters of rooms) where the babies incubated. Charlie's first pod was the J-pod. Nurses were typically assigned two babies at a time, and they tried to pair them up so that the nurse had at least one easy baby, a grow and gain kid who was stable but needed fattening, like a goose. This left him or her more attention for the "hard" baby, the one who needed help with any or all of the major life-supporting functions: breathing, eating, regulating temperature. Charlie was always a hard one.

Once I found my pod for the day, I'd wash my hands for a minimum of two minutes with special soap, from the elbows down with the tiny disposable brush as the diagram indicated. And then each time I exited and reentered his room, I added a dollop of the hand sanitizer mounted on the wall. I think I lost a layer of skin after all was said and done. My hands looked like rancher's, tough and cracked but very clean. When I close my eyes, I can still smell the antiseptic scent of alcohol and aloe. It lives in a memory bank separate from cut grass and pumpkin bread. Its friends are the first poop after switching your kid to solids and vomited hot dog.

I was surprised the first time they rolled me into Charlie's room. Someone had already made a sign on his windows that spelled his name in little laminated sunshines. A volunteer had also already dropped off a hand-knit cap and a tiny square of flannel for a blanket. I wondered, as I traced the outline of a car on the soft fabric, if these people had been screened. They weren't on our VIP list. How did I know they remembered to scrub in the right direction? It was a weird feeling, this knowledge that other people had a gateway to my son and were already doing the mothering.

Of course, none of this was much like the picture I held of Charlie's first days out in the wide world. This plastic incubator with tubes snaking into his mouth and nose was nothing like the white crib with the antique finish that awaited him at home. These pale walls were not the aqua color with the cheerful name from the Disney collection. Not even a day old and he had IVs in his leg and arm. We were so afraid to touch him that first early morning. There wasn't much to touch, just a peak of a nose and eyes over a bundle that was mostly wires. But we did place our sterile, shaking hands on him, rest them there for a moment so he could feel our warmth and impart some kind of humanity. If I had any mothering instincts at this time, this went against all of them. The minute I touched him, I wanted more. This was the beginning of an addiction. He should be in my arms, on my chest, making noises. He should not be in a box, separate from us, hooked up to a machine that looked like it was stealing rather than giving breaths. Other people's blankets should not cover his feet.

Charlie's first few days were a hard transition for us from one group set apart to another. We had felt the sting of being the "infertile couple," but "NICU parents" was even worse. I was still staying with all the other new mothers in the maternity ward. We would smile and grimace at each other while pacing the halls, reminding our bodies how to perambulate. But that was where the camaraderie ended. They wore matching pajamas and robes. They had packed a makeup kit and shampoo. They had balloons and a new baby in their room. I wore my college sweatpants and a cardigan because that was all I could grab in the darkness of our midnight drive. My hair was greasy and legs unshaved. We had packed no hospital bag because we were supposed to have two and a half more months. Even I wasn't that proactive. There was no baby in the room because he was still supposed to be in my belly. The other mothers practiced nursing with a lactation consultant, who heard their complaints like a priest sitting confession. Meanwhile, I was hooking myself up to a hospital-grade high-powered pumping machine. My breasts turned to udders while that "liquid gold" that was breast milk was extracted. Please don't get me started on the pressure for NICU (and all) mothers to breastfeed. From the pump down the tubes into the canisters and into the freezer—already there were too many elements between myself and my child. I was on the outside tapping on the glass, impatiently waiting to be let in. I was a mom, but not the mom I had prayed to be.

My first true meltdown did not happen until I was released from the hospital and had to leave Charlie behind. He had been with me for months and months. We had a nice thing going. I wasn't ready to say good-bye, even for a few hours. I wasn't ready to sleep away from him. Jody and I got lost in the parking garage. I cried and wanted to claw at the upholstery of the car because it felt like God didn't want us to leave either. Everything was heavy with omens. But we did leave. We went home and I went straight to Charlie's room. I opened the drawers to his dresser that had taken so long to assemble that Christmas Day an eternity ago and pulled out a monogrammed onesie and socks, a gauze blanket, a hat. He couldn't use any of it. He was still too small for the outfit and the IVs prohibited adornment. I just wanted something in the metal drawer below his incubator. I wanted a piece of that room to hold the promise of home. And when I woke in the night to keep up the pumping every four hours, I cried and tried to picture him, one day here with me, when this separation would be a distant memory.

When Sarah, formerly the beautiful seducer of kings, was finally blessed with Isaac, she said, "God has brought me laughter, and everyone who hears about this will laugh with me" (Genesis 21:6). Do you think Abraham told this woman, this fierce mama, God's orders to "Take your son, your only son, Isaac, whom you love, and go to the region of Moriah. Sacrifice him there as a burnt offering on one of the mountains I will tell you about" (Genesis 22:2)? There's a reason she is conspicuously absent from this part of the story. Abraham would never have made it out alive if she'd known. And Hannah, our formerly barren wife of Elkanah, greedily clung to her time with baby Samuel before dedicating him to God. "After the boy is weaned," she bargained, "I will take him and present him before the Lord, and he will live there always" (1 Samuel 1:22). If there was ever a case for breastfeeding into toddlerhood, it would be this. Mothers do not let go gently.

The length of the NICU stay is indeterminate. Some babies are out and home in a matter of days. They might have been a little jaundiced or needed extra practice eating. Some babies can stay eight months or longer if they are immunocompromised or on a ventilator. Some babies simply "graduate" to the pediatric intensive care unit (PICU) after a year has passed and their disease/disorder persists. We did not know where Charlie fell on the sliding scale. As the doctors and nurses loved to say whenever I tried to pin someone down on a time frame, "There is no crystal ball" to predict the outcome. Here's what we did know: He was on a ventilator to help him breathe, but on lower and lower doses of oxygen and pressure, which was a good sign. His blood sugars were stable. He appeared symmetrical—one leg wasn't dangling longer than the other. Organs were measuring within normal range. But he did have those pits and creases in his ears and, of course, the protruding tongue. He looked like a tiny mischievous elf with piercings.

I would stand at his incubator and covet, covet the child

that was mine by all rights. It didn't seem fair that I couldn't reach in, pluck him out, and take him home. So he's small? So he sticks out his tongue? Big deal! But it was a big deal. And the monitors that consistently alarmed the second he was no longer intubated were reminders enough to shatter any kind of illusion of health. He could not breathe very long on his own. He would be fine for a few minutes, but then begin to pant, tongue out and tiny chest heaving with effort, while his rib cage made itself known, birdlike and apparent. He had a nasal gastric tube: a tiny hollow tube like a flexible straw that ran through his nose and into his stomach, where my breast milk would trickle. We couldn't begin to think of a bottle, much less breastfeeding, when he couldn't even suck down air. I remember the first time I held him. It took twenty minutes and a lifetime to get him and all his tubes out of the incubator and into my arms. He weighed almost nothing. He was a warm bundle of blankets, like socks from the dryer. My arms were sore for days because I had held him so stiffly, afraid to dislodge a wire, some vital piece to him.

Sometime during my hospital stay, spring had fully arrived and the late March weather stayed windy and warm. My days began to take on shape. I still woke to the internal teacher's clock and had a passing recognition of each class period rolling over to the next, like a moment of silence in church. But while my students were working through a new novel with a new teacher, I was timing my half-hour drives to the NICU to coincide with pumpings and tube feedings and temperature checks and diaper changes. If I had to learn to be a mother and a nurse, so be it. I would arrive toting freshly pumped milk in a little cooler for them to put on ice. I actually buckled it in, checking the strap was nice and snug. I needn't have been so concerned. We eventually had to make an impromptu trip to H. H. Gregg to buy a deep freeze because we had used up our allotted freezer space at the hospital. I knew other NICU moms desperately drinking herbal teas and massaging mammaries to increase production. I was a fertility goddess in this one respect. My body knew how to churn out milk, like a slightly neurotic dairy cow. Don't think I didn't stop and thank the Lord for this one small blessing on our behalf.

Once in the inner sanctum of the NICU, and after dropping off my cache and scrubbing down, I would get to participate in Charlie's "care routine." I'd change his tiny diaper, a napkin really, check his temperature under his arm, and then hold the little nasal tube while gravity let my milk flow into his stomach. If his oxygen didn't drop during the feeding, they would let me hold him. I would talk to him ... mostly about me and his dad and his room and George Orwell's *1984*. It was the last thing I was teaching before labor and perhaps not suitable for naptime, but he seemed to be the most relaxed during these nonsense talks. So I discussed Big Brother and newspeak and why women in overalls were a big deal. I tried to get into female empowerment one day, but he dozed at the first mention of Sonia Sotomayor. I would leave each visit exhausted, but already setting my phone alarm for our next rendezvous in three hours. While not your standard caretaking, I craved it. I could not get my fill of him.

It was Jesus' family tradition to travel to Jerusalem for the Feast of the Passover. He'd been doing it all His life. But when He was twelve, after the feast, His parents left and He did not. This is the best "never leave your child unattended" story.

This isn't losing your toddler in the aisles at Target for a minute or leaving your house with all the diaper bags and none of the kids. His parents left Him and went on their merry way "for a day" (Luke 2:44). A day, people. That's like *Home Alone*, hop a plane to France, territory. I suppose that proves Jesus had an unassuming childhood. When they finally realized He was missing, they did what any self-respecting parents would do: Turn around and travel back to the last place they'd seen Him. Back to Jerusalem. If we're doing the math, that's a weekend's worth of days for an unsupervised Jesus.

When they finally spotted Him, He was "in the temple courts, sitting among the teachers, listening to them and asking questions" (Luke 2:46). I cannot begin to imagine Mary and Joseph's irritation when they see Him, not scared and searching for Mom and Dad, but hanging out, chatting. Children are responsible for the erosion of all our mental shores. Mary asked (and I will let you insert whatever tone you find appropriate), "Son, why have you treated us like this? Your father and I have been anxiously searching for you" (Luke 2:48). Anxiously. Searching. Mary might ponder this one in her heart later, but right now she's frazzled and tired. Her son responds: "Why were you searching for me? Didn't you know I had to be in my Father's house?" (Luke 2:49). Oh, the cheek of Him.

Mary and Joseph "did not understand what he was saying to them" (Luke 2:50). The idea of giving up those parental controls was unthinkable, even to those two, who saw the bigger picture more than most. But Jesus reminded them, often and to the very end, that they had to let go. Eventually Hannah had to stop nursing Samuel and take him to Shiloh, to the temple. She had to kneel before God, perhaps with her hand on her son's small back, feeling his heartbeat, and she had to say, "I prayed for this child, and the Lord has granted me what I asked of him. So now I give him to the Lord. For his whole life he will be given over to the Lord" (1 Samuel 1:26–28).

It is such an odd thing to learn that our children are not our own. For most, the letting go comes slowly: first day of kindergarten, driver's license, off to college, marriage. It is a gentle unraveling of the apron strings. But for me, from the very beginning, God drew back the curtain on the illusions of ownership in motherhood. Whatever motherhood might look like for you through pregnancy, surrogacy, fostering, adopting, or mentoring, through infancy, toddlerhood, threenagers, and teenagers, it is all a process of letting go. It is a continual reminder that we cannot claim possession of either our lives or the lives of those we love.

Charlie belonged first to God, and I was blessed to be the servant to care for His child. I was to treat Charlie like the gift he was, not with greed and fear of loss, but with amazement that he was mine to look after. It was not a lesson I took to kindly. It still takes learning, as I remain vigilant, always protective of his world. But his was a collective upbringing from the start. They say it takes a village. And Charlie's village was bigger than most: mom and dad, grandparents, friends, pastors, doctors, nurses, respiratory therapists, and even volunteers. We all chipped in until he could thrive on his own.

Motherhood can close you off. It can seal the doors shut on your heart in an effort of self- and family preservation. You want to keep your world safe, insulated in hyperalertness and Rosie the Riveter arms. But we cannot save ourselves. That's the point. We have to let others into the hurt and the hopes. More than anything else at the time, I prayed to be grateful for this alien invasion of our budding family because it reminded me to stay open. And most days, Lord willing, it works.

Guiding Questions

1. How, as Jesus reminds His mother, might you practice viewing the people in your life as gifts rather than possessions? How would this new outlook change the way you love those closest to you?
2. How could you let someone into your "village" today to help you where you need it most?

Scripture

- Luke 2:41–51
- Genesis 21:6, 22:2
- 1 Samuel 1:22–28

Chapter 18

"The Pressure" and the Widow with Two Coins

Man, the widows in the Bible have it rough. Let's say you are happily married in Merry Old Israel when suddenly your husband dies, maybe in battle, or maybe in famine, or maybe the plague got him. Let's also say you have no children. Maybe you two had not yet had "the talk" about whether you were ready to "start trying." Or maybe you are barren, since women in that era tended to swing toward one extreme (a litter) or the other (none). Now you're all on your own, and if you're lucky, you've got a sheep or two and some land. However, you have no one to herd those sheep or work that land so you watch as it slowly goes to seed and maybe a wolf carries off your last lamb. Your options are as follows: (1) Find a kinsman-redeemer to marry you. This could be your husband's brother or closest male relative. (2) Return to your homeland, begin the process of dowry gathering again, put on some mascara, and pray that you are young enough to attract someone new. (3) Seek out refuge near the temple and beg, hoping someone will take pity and do their due diligence to "give proper recognition to those widows who are really in need" (I Timothy 5:3).

There was a reason the woman at the well was living with

a man not her husband and the widow of Zarephath did not readily offer Elijah food and water. There was a reason Naomi gave Ruth and Orpah the option to go home again and start fresh. Widowhood was not for the faint of heart. You had to be tough to cobble together a life.

That is why the scene of the widow who gives her last two coins is so powerful. Jesus has taken up a perch near the place in the temple where people drop their offerings. I imagine Him a little to one side, so as not to draw attention to Himself, but still close enough to get a clear view of the transfer of goods. According to the story, "Many rich people threw in large amounts" (Mark 12:41). I was raised in the Southern, Protestant way of discreetly folding your check or bills and placing them in the offering basket as inconspicuously as possible. The amount rendered should be nobody's business but God's. Of course, as a kid, I brought a dollar from my allowance to put in on my own, which I always managed to do with a flourish, like Dame Judi Dench dropping a hanky. It was partly the thrill of partaking in such a grown-up event, but it was also that need for each good deed to be noted, even then. I am forever a hoarder of approval.

In the story of the widow with her coins, a plethora of rich people drop off piles of coins and fatted calves and expensive rugs and jugs of perfume—with a flourish. And then a poor widow walks up. I envision her old and vaguely resembling Mother Teresa, but she could just as easily be twenty and buxom. Widows come in all shapes and sizes and ages after all. She plunks down two coins, not even the equivalent of a penny. Jesus beckons over His disciples, always at the ready, and says, "I tell you the truth, this poor widow has put more into the treasury than all the others. They all gave out of their wealth; but she, out of her poverty, put everything in—all she had to live on" (Mark 12:43–44).

All she had to live on. She may not have looked like Mother Teresa, but she was Mother Teresa in deed. And people near the edges probably snickered. Maybe it was the rich who were still packing up their emptied baskets and winding up their slack sheep leashes. More likely, it was the middle class looking to make themselves feel better. It's the middle child who needs the most reassurance. The widow did her thing anyway and Jesus took note.

It is almost impossible for me to imagine being in her position and just letting go, jumping without a net. As Jody and I watched Charlie struggle to breathe each time he was taken off the ventilator and as we counted the seconds or minutes, or if it was a good day, hours, between breathing spells, I prayed for dear life, literally for dear life. How, I caught myself wondering, was I in the exact same position praying the same prayer that I had through years of trying to get pregnant? Why was "life" so hard to conjure and keep? In the meantime, I held on to everything I could that made me feel grounded. It was a blessed and cursed policy that you could phone the NICU at any time of the day or night to get a report on your child. We always called at night, right before we went to sleep, and around 2 or 3 a.m. when I was up pumping, and again around 6 a.m. for a last report from the night nurse before shift change. We prayed for two spells or less between phone calls. Sometimes, however, he stopped breathing half a dozen times a night before they decided to give the kid a break and let him sleep it out on the ventilator. I had started to make notations in my planner each day that consisted of the number of spells, units of breastmilk ingested, and the rate of air flow and amount of oxygen on the ventilator. I yearned for a pattern, an upward trend to keep me...up. I needed a hit of optimism.

Among all this uncertainty, however, we were comforted by the fact that Beckwith-Wiedemann syndrome is a syndrome with primarily physical impacts. His noggin, his intellect, was A-okay as the brain scan at seven days old had confirmed. So if we could just get him past the immediate danger of the next days, weeks, or heaven forbid, months, then we could get on with life. After all, the majority of BWS kids end up entirely normal adults with minimal lasting side effects. That's why most of the doctors and nurses, and especially anyone in the nonmedical world, looked at us with blank stares when we told them his diagnosis. Nobody spends money to research a syndrome that ultimately leads to a completely normal life. Talk about anticlimactic.

And Charlie was trending up! Cue the cymbals and popping corks and hurrahs! After weeks of experimenting on and off the ventilator, he was off, permanently. They didn't wheel it out of the room or anything, but it was shoved to the corner like the guy at the party nobody wants to talk to. And despite continuing episodes where his oxygen level dropped, he was bringing them back up himself. The kid was finally catching on. He lost a few wires and grew rounder. With the removal of IVs, I began to put little socks on him. I had also special-ordered Velcro outfits that I maneuvered over the sticky leads on his belly. He was a vision in rubber ducky yellow. The clothes drawer was being put to good use. We began to give him tastes of breast milk on his pacifier and then through a syringe-sized bottle. He ate greedily. But not well. He usually had a spell after this whenever we increased the amount. But increase we did. He would lie on his side on my knee and hold my thumb with his whole hand, like a monkey, and suck and breathe and suck and breathe and it felt a bit of normal.

There really is no "normal" in the NICU, though. If you've hit normal, you go home. The NICU is like riding Willy Wonka's glass elevator to Miss Peregrine's orphanage. The longer you stay, the more your world turns topsy-turvy. One month in, and I had arrived for the first bottle-feeding, diaper-changing, temp-taking session. We had a new nurse that day. I walked in, ready to make small talk, the kind you develop especially for the NICU: "Nice out today! Wish these windows opened . . . ha ha ha." "Definitely needed the extra coffee this morning. I don't know how the night nurses do it. Cheers!" I wouldn't get to deliver any of my lines that morning. The new nurse cut to the quick. I had just missed rounds. The head of intensive care wanted to speak with me regarding some test results. She'd page him to see if he was still in this pod. Was my husband here today? she asked.

It's never good news when the doctor in charge wants to talk to you. The goal is to keep a low profile and hope you can bail your kid out ASAP. But I was waving at Charlie and focusing on setting out his little diaper and change of clothes. In other words, I was doing my mothering when the doctor came in. He was followed by seven other people holding clipboards. I had stopped reading their nametags long ago. The head of the NICU was an older, gray-haired man with a slightly rounded middle, the exact kind of person you want in

charge of all the babies. He looked welcoming yet astute—
Santa, if he'd gone to medical school. I can recall only bits
and pieces of the conversation that followed. Trauma will do
that to you. I remember I was holding Charlie at the time
and the nurse had to take him from me because I was crying and shaking and swaying like a shoddy mast. They tried
to make me sit down, but I'm a fidgeter. I pace when I get
upset. I remember being made to study a printout of the new
brain scan done at thirty days. I remember gray and black
and the big pools of white that shouldn't be there, potholes in
the pavement. He lined up the seven-day ultrasound next to
it, using a pen he pulled from his pocket to point to the tiny
dots that they had not taken much notice of until now. Those
dots had morphed into cysts and what would lead to a term I
could, in later years, repeat ten times fast: *periventricular leu-
komalacia* (PVL). Twelve syllables that meant one thing: damage in all four quadrants of the brain.

I kissed Charlie, whom the nurse was now holding, on
his small, slightly antiseptic-smelling head, walked out of
the hospital, got in my car, drove home...and fell to pieces.
I called Jody, ending a time in his life when he was not the
father of a son with brain damage, and then refused to meet
him back at the hospital. He could go hear it from the doctor, but I couldn't bear it again. I wept and railed. Oh, how
I railed against the unfairness. I broke things and clutched
at my clothes, like they were the problem. I marched in circles. I scared the dog. We had fought for this child, Jody and
me. We had fought infertility for years and we had lost and
we had won and now, not only would our son have to fight
to breathe, to eat, to speak, but he would now also have to

fight to understand the world around him, to understand the differences that separated him from his peers, differences that would not be outgrown. We knew he would have special needs. But why all of them? I was emptied out and alone, sitting on the floor of his room and refusing to talk to God. I could not have prayed even if I'd wanted to.

The morning drifted into afternoon and I drove back to the hospital with my milk, sure it would not have the same sweet taste it held before. Jody was still there. It was the second time in my life I'd seen him really cry. He met me in the corridor and let out big anguished, can't-catch-your-breath sobs. I did not. We held each other and then I held Charlie. But I couldn't make my arms work properly. I had nothing to give anyone, not grief or compassion. But I could still feed and change and cradle and so I did. I was a mostly functioning body whose spirit had drifted.

The doctor, Jody would later tell me, had been emphatic in his "we don't have a crystal ball" approach. Some kids with PVL might have a slight limp or have trouble with certain levels of math. It didn't have to mean wheelchairs and drooling. Another doctor on rounds—we had many—called up a developmental specialist and handed the phone to me despite my waving it away like a grenade. He just stood there, holding it out and repeating, "Here, you need to talk to her," until I had no choice. "Ask her your questions," he prompted. This doctor was excellent in his treatment of patients and later became our favorite, but he ran a little short on the social skills. He was a steamroller of good intentions. The first thing I asked this stranger, the expert at the other end of the line, was if Charlie would be able to walk, given this new news. She answered like she was leaning into the phone, aggressively, that I should be more concerned with his cognitive abilities and whether he would talk. I needed to get my priorities straight, so to speak. I hung up aggressively. There are some people you can choose not to let into your life. Some people don't get to walk through your gate.

In certain seasons, God gives you ample time and space to get angry, to grieve, to approach each level of the process- ing process systematically. And sometimes your world just implodes. Motherhood can often feel like this. The pressure builds with no release until suddenly there's nowhere else for the hurt or exhaustion or frustration to go. Someone is sitting on the release valve. It was the same for me in these early weeks. Not long after Charlie's new diagnosis, his breathing spells began to increase. I was no longer allowed to feed him by mouth and they reinserted the nasal gastric tube. They increased the amount of times he was given "blow-by," oxygen held over his mouth or nose to perk him up, like smelling salts or a shot of whiskey. As they held the mask a few inches from Charlie's face, I would watch him go from ashy to pale to rosy and finally understand why casinos pump in that extra oxy- gen. You're high on life.

By now we had grown certain that the source of Charlie's distress was his severely enlarged tongue. We had hoped that time would give him the strength and skill to work around it. The waiting game, however, was proving ineffectual and now unsafe. See how many gumballs you can fit in your mouth and then try to take a deep breath and you'll know what I mean. Skill can get you only so far. So we tried work-arounds. The ear, nose, and throat (ENT) doctor inserted nasal trumpets on several occasions, which looked exactly like they sound. They were little flexible rubber tubes that went down each nostril and into the throat and flared at the opening of the nose, like petunias. He would be okay for minutes or hours with these in and we'd convince ourselves we'd found the magic cure, but then he'd tire out and the tubes would be removed so oxygen could be administered. We were moving backward, not forward. We did two endoscopies to see where his tongue ended and how much space existed between it and the tonsils and adenoids. By mid-May, two months into our NICU stay, we still had no answers.

The call came in the middle of the night, but went unheard, a rare miss when we were both too deep in exhausted slumber. In the morning, I got the message and broke it to Jody. By a fluke, I had become the perpetual bearer of bad news. Charlie had had a "rough night." There had been eight episodes of prolonged apnea. Several where he turned blue. One spectacular doozy had required reinforcements: one nurse to hold him upside down while the other used a tongue depressor to pry his tongue from the roof of his mouth and administer oxygen. He was now intubated again after over a month off the ventilator and, they warned, had an IV line running from his head. So don't panic when you see him.

My life had become one long, slow panic.

The widow with the coins practiced how to live without holding on too tightly. She really had nothing left to hold on to anyway. We do not know where she slept at night. Was it outside in the cold on the temple steps or in some kind soul's stable? We do not know the last time she ate a real meal. Days maybe? There's an image I carry in my head when I think of the rich at this time in history. It is of Scrooge McDuck in *DuckTales*, when he slides down his mountain of gold in his ducky mansion.

Two coins couldn't even make a hill. She let them fall. I'd like to think she was hopeful in that last small gesture. Here, let me do some good, before I've got none left to do. I'd be the skeleton they uncover in shipwrecks, still clutching that strand of pearls in my bony fingers.

When I saw Charlie, tiny and immobilized again, it was the end for me all over again. God had no goodness to offer me, nor me Him. We were done.

My spirit had never fully returned from the news of the brain scan, maybe not even from the news from that first ultrasound in January, which showed something was awry. This was the kick that sent me sprawling. We were trending so far down that I could no longer see light.

The one thing I did do, begrudgingly, during this time was let Jody pray for us. I sat in physical attendance, if nothing else, while he prayed that God would keep Charlie protected and deliver him to us in whatever state He saw fit. Looking back, I like to think that was a version of throwing my two coins in by proxy.

Sometimes you cannot work your way out. Sometimes the ache and disappointment and fear are too sharp to see past. Sometimes you will not respond with appropriate trust in God.

It's okay.

Let me say it again: It's okay.

You will not always be the widow who let go.

Guiding Questions

1. When have you been "a functioning body whose spirit has drifted," simply going through the motions of your life? What advice would you give someone in that place?
2. Whom do you trust to throw your two coins in "by proxy"?

Scripture

- 1 Timothy 5:3
- Mark 12:41–43

Chapter 19

"The Upside" and God's Humor

Believe it or not, there were a few not so serious happenings during our time in the NICU. Not everything was darkness and despair. You can cry only so much before things swing around and become amusing again in a trippy kind of way. It's the premise of dark comedies and almost all stand-up routines. God knows our limits and sneaks in the peaks among the valleys. He lightens the yoke before our knees buckle. Even in infertility there were laughable moments. I ate Push Pops in January on our snow-covered deck while the hormones burned me up from the inside out. And I tried to keep a straight face while my RE made the abstinence speech during many of the two-week waits. Was he worried we'd slip up and get pregnant? And in motherhood, the comedic relief is endless . . . poop on walls, toys in toilets, erasers up noses, selfie haircuts. You laugh even as you want to scream a little. Even after Charlie's recent diagnosis and his increased breathing spells, I could still acknowledge the laughable moments, even if I wasn't in a laughing mood.

There's this knowledge in the NICU, once you've been there awhile, been around the block, or pod, if you will, of a hierarchy of rooms. There are certain rooms you just do not want. Avoid the small rooms. These offer the same allure as tiny houses. They seem cute and convenient in the beginning until you realize you don't actually want to sleep in a loft bed overlooking the toilet, which is cozied up next to the kitchen sink . . . even if it is on wheels.

Even larger rooms might not be your best bet if you get one that hasn't been upgraded since the big remodel. Hospitals, children's hospitals especially, are always remodeling. There will forever be a better configuration of pods or sink arrangements or stars or fish or monkeys on the ceiling. Research says so. The non-upgraded room has the rocking chair that doesn't rock. It looks like it should, but it's a lie. It will play you for a fool every time. It also has the curtains that don't pull all the way around for privacy, like the dress you think will fit, but zips up only to your bra line. The rooms are designed to be seen from every angle for safety purposes. You need an eye on those babies at all times. But some smarty intuited that parents might not actually want to feel like animals on display all the time. Curtains were hung for privacy. Yet by some mismeasurement or psychological experiment, some curtains did not reach all the way across the room. That bra was just gonna have to show. Try hooking yourself up to the breast pump in that environment. It's like prison, no safe way to turn your back.

The good rooms are the big ones—the prime suites that could be two rooms and sometimes are if the NICU is over capacity. And the king of all rooms, the win-the-lottery penthouse, is the big room with a wall of windows at the back that overlooks the downtown skyline. This room has a chair that rocks, curtains that close, space to move, and natural daylight—a thing almost unheard of on the medical scene. You could live the agrarian life if you wanted to, ignoring the clock and letting the sun tell you noon from night. There is a peacefulness to this room that the others cannot offer. It almost makes you forget where you are. Almost.

I arrived one day to find the NICU almost to capacity, full to the brim with babies. I groaned, inwardly and outwardly, knowing it would be a scavenger hunt to find Charlie, and feeling a little guilty that I wasn't more saddened by all the new little people that had landed upon hard times. I followed the red circles to the orange moons to the nurse who had been there that fated day of the brain scan. She walked me to Charlie's new placement. Glory be, it was the big room. It was still early morning and the sun was streaming in, albeit on the heart rate monitor, but still, sunshine! After pulling the curtains that reached all the way like a hug, I did a very quiet and quick touchdown dance and then called Jody with the good news. Insurance was finally paying off and it put us at the Hilton. I sat down in that rocking chair with Charlie and enjoyed the view. He looked up at me with this face like, *See, Mom, I got your back.* He's smooth like that.

As you walk by, sizing up the rooms, you can't help but peek in on the other cohabitants. You hope to catch baby sounds, cries, coos, hiccups, anything human is nice to hear over the sucking noises and beeps of machines. You try not to feel like a rubbernecker at a car crash. And you cannot help but read each name pasted to the windows. Remember, Charlie's name had been written in little sunshines that danced across the wall, and those suns moved with him to all of his various rooms. Many of the names I spied were better than a *New Yorker* cartoon, once you got the joke. There was a "Precious Moments" and a "Princess Barbie," and a "Bodacious" in case you missed the eighties. Also, if you were peckish, there was a "Lasagna" and a "Chardonnay." I rarely looked in on the parents, because eye contact was a faux pas with anyone other than your nurse or doctor, but they either had a really good sense of humor or knew their baby would need one. If any kid could handle being named Lasagna, it would be a kid who beat the NICU.

All jokes aside, there was this one time when I got pulled over for speeding. You're thinking I already told this story, right? Nope. New day, new cop, new speed limit broken. I am better now. I swear. Children slow you down in ways I did not know was possible. So this time around I was on the interstate on my way to the NICU with my trusty insulated bag of breast milk in the passenger seat. Charlie's care times when he ate were etched in stone. If you missed your window, you were out of luck until the next go-around. Now here's where I admit I wasn't running late. I'm rarely late. Perhaps it is the speeding? On this particular April morning, I had no reason to speed. But I do like to go fast. It's not crazy, dangerous, drag-racing territory, but a touch above the norm feels right, just to edge out of the pack. Well, I had just nosed ahead when a motorcycle cop pulled out from the underpass and got me, sirens a-wailing.

He pulled me over and sat. He was talking into the radio that was perched on his shoulder like a parrot. He was my personal pirate. Then he sat some more. Then he whipped out what had to be an iPhone and scrolled for upwards of five minutes. Was he playing Candy Crush back there? As time and other cars passed, I began to get anxious. I did not want to miss this feeding. It was around that crucial time when we were trying to get Charlie to take more by mouth and wean him off the tube. Like sand shifting under your feet, I felt it, slowly but surely losing my composure. By the time he approached my window, I was a heaving, new-mom torrent of hormones. I might have drooled on myself a little. He was unmoved. He didn't even take the sunglasses off.

After the expected, "Do you know how fast you were going back there, ma'am?" he asked me if I had any good reason to go that fast. He asked it with the attitude of a teacher who knows the kid is going to have no excuse for not doing his homework. I know that act. I've done it. But because he had taken his sweet time issuing the citation, I was most definitely going to be late and now had a very legitimate reason for crying. I told him, in between hiccups, that I was on my way to feed my son, who was in the NICU. A beat of three seconds, and then he asked for proof. How do I show him the absence of a baby? If there is someone out there in the wide world who would lie about the NICU to get out of a ticket, I do not want to meet them. I wasn't about to open up my insulated containers of milk. It seemed a contamination to let him even set eyes on them. So I whipped out my NICU armband and gave him the phone number and my son's name, vaguely wondering if this could somehow go on Charlie's permanent record.

He ended up letting me go with a warning and a lecture on how I, "of all people," should understand the importance of safety and protecting the other families on the road. He was good. It was worse than a ticket. After he walked away, I patted the milk in the passenger seat and apologized. But here's where it gets really good. When I rushed into the hospital, out of breath and way past feeding time with my guilty milk, a round of applause broke out from the nurses' station. "Glad to see you're not in jail," they said. "We almost told him we didn't know you." Apparently, before letting me go, he had actually called to verify my story. By now the nurses and I had a very casual relationship. Teasing was fair game. They laughed. I laughed, suddenly very glad I had been supplying them with a steady flow of baked goods over the weeks. They had informed Charlie's nurse I was on my way. She had waited for me to feed him. We were in this big game of life together.

Sometime, it must have been early on because we were still in our first tiny room, someone decided it would be a good idea to let "Mom give him a bath." I could reinsert a nasal gastric tube, no problem, but the idea of immersing him in water terrified me. For one thing, they have to unhook him from all his probes. For a small window of time, he was just a baby in need of a bath. There were no monitors reading his heart rate or oxygen levels. He was a free man. But I did not know how to take care of a baby without the machines. It felt so off the grid. But when they wheeled in the little yellow tub filled with warm water, they didn't really give me a choice. "I've already disconnected the leads," the nurse said, handing me a naked Charlie. How can something so medically fragile flail like a weasel? I lassoed him in my arms as best I could. He wiggled and peed. The nurse flanked my side, and we lowered him into the two inches of water. That first bath. It was so oddly normal once we got started. Despite the big tongue, he was like any kid, splashing and kicking and sucking the washcloth for all he was worth. We actually had to take the washcloth away. He was sucking so hard, he was turning a little blue. It didn't matter that this was a small, windowless room. I wasn't looking anywhere but at him at that moment, his slick pooched belly and huge blue eyes, like wells. I have a picture from that first bath. I'm holding up a damp and bundled Charlie like the Stanley Cup. He was clean. We were victorious.

It is rare to make good friends in later life, and the NICU typically isn't where you go looking. After college and especially after marriage, you tend to settle into your ways. After high school, college, new jobs, dating, and marriage, you're kind of done with the mingling scene. Sure, you have plenty of acquaintances, but friends that you make time for are rare so you pick from the oldies but goodies. You've already made the effort with them. They're locked in.

If new friends are hard, new best friends are nearly impossible. We don't really even use that term much once we reach our thirties, do we? It sounds so childish, like you should be buying matching heart necklaces at Claire's. But God managed to land me a best friend in the NICU. She was, if you can believe it, that nurse who paged the head doctor and stood witness on one of the worst days of my life, the PVL day. Not an auspicious start to a friendship. But if a friend is someone who loves you at your worst, we had a good thing going. She's also the one who gave me the best room later on, so there's that. Her name is Mary, and like all the other good Marys, she's awesome on a biblical level. We did not know we would become friends. But because she was the calmest and most competent caretaker who also happened to share my dry sense of humor, we asked her to be Charlie's "primary" nurse. This meant that if she was scheduled to work, they would automatically assign her to Charlie. He was hard. You couldn't coast on a Charlie shift. This was a serious pledge, but we had our "define the relationship" talk and she agreed to commit.

The first time that Mary and I discussed anything other than Charlie was when I arrived to find her with a wicked sunburn. Her neighborhood pool had opened the day before. She had fallen asleep sans sunscreen. Of all people to forget sunscreen, a nurse. Although given the number of nurses and doctors who also take smoke breaks, I think we can assume they are not above the common vices. She moved very slowly that day. It looked like it hurt to breathe, and she could not fully raise or lower her arms. She smelled like aloe and coconut. This was so exactly something I would do. Which meant that I listened to her complain about the pain and then mocked her incessantly. Perhaps our love language is calamity? She also had a profound effect on Charlie too, or at least his bowels. He managed to have a blowout diaper almost every time she was near. I never saw her in the same scrubs after lunch. Apparently, she had a relaxing effect on us all. For all this, I have Charlie to thank.

If there was ever anything straight from God, it is the synergistic relationship that Mary, her husband, Jody, and I have fallen into over the years. We have celebrated Thanksgivings and New Years and Fourth of Julys and almost every birthday for which I have been recruited to make the dessert. We have eaten chili and watched football. We have seen *Harry Potter* at the symphony because we are proud geeks. We have picnicked and drunk wine at a vineyard. We have traded books and Netflix queues. These are our people. How does God work such a miracle when you didn't even know it was a miracle you needed? I'm pretty sure David had a line for Jonathan that went something like . . . "It was the beginning of a beautiful friendship."

From the "good room" to the motorcycle cop to the creative baby names to the friends, we had our share of laughter. And I would come to see that more and more as time passed and the distance grew from our NICU life. God has a sense of humor and genius comedic timing. Let us not forget Balaam's donkey chatting him up or adolescent Jesus lecturing His parents or Sarah seducing Pharaohs while Abraham watched. We need a bit of levity. Don't worry. God knows. It will be there when you least expect it. You might feel like you've lost that part of yourself that used to laugh for no reason. But she's still in there. Trust me.

Guiding Questions

1. When have you seen God's humor in unexpected places?
2. Who is someone that God brought into your life when you least expected it, and most needed it?
3. What's the last thing you laughed out loud about?

Scripture

- Numbers 22:21–39
- Luke 2:41–52
- Genesis 12:10–16

Chapter 20

"The Exit Strategy" and Samson's Mom

After Charlie's upside-down, tongue-depressing, bagging incident, it became clear to us and all of his treatment team that the status quo was not cutting it. He wasn't growing into that tongue. In fact, the weight gain and growth had served only to feed the beast. It was growing faster than he was. If we were ever going to get out of the NICU, at eight weeks and counting, we were going to have to take drastic measures. How much more extreme could it get? What is more drastic than a ventilator in the NICU? But there was one more option, Plan X or Y way down on the list—the thing the residents stopped talking about whenever we drew near. But on one gorgeous day in May that had all the students in all the schools dreaming of summer and all the birds in all the trees trumpeting spring, they started talking. And we started listening, as our ENT with the Scooby Doo tie explained the risks and benefits of a tracheotomy.

The slang term for your trachea is "windpipe." This makes sense. It's how the breath, the wind, gets pushed in and out of you. Charlie's tongue was one big clog in the pipe, like an unmoving mass of goop in the drain. Nothing was getting past that sucker, not even air. It's also why eating wore him out so much. How do you suck, swallow, and breathe, when each of these tasks requires open space in an already cramped corridor? You knock out a wall. Which is what a tracheotomy would do. We could bypass the tongue and open up the windpipe at a different place. Easy-peasy! The surgeon would simply cut a horizontal hole in Charlie's windpipe, puncture what nature made whole, insert a plastic tube, and then tie it in place with Velcro, like a dog's collar. How could I, how could any parent, opt for this? How do you even begin to make that kind of decision? Up to now, all the big stuff had been left to the professionals. We barely knew how to parent with what little responsibility they gave us. We were amateurs.

We stood in the hallway outside Charlie's room, where you couldn't see the sun or hear the birds or feel anything other than the intensity of the intensive care. I tried to pretend I was a rational human being, the kind I used to be who brushed her teeth and made pro and con lists. I tried to really hear the words as our ENT spoke. But all I could do was watch his Scooby Doo tie bob up and down, riding his Adam's apple like a horse.

To understand the tie, you'd have to understand the man. He was an offbeat mix of jocularity and seriousness. Each time he rounded, I waited for the tie. He had Batman and Homer Simpson and Goofy and flying pigs. The tie was the highlight of my day. My world had gotten very small. So I kept my eyes on Scooby Doo while words like "incision," "stoma," "tracheotomy tube," and "suction machine" flitted in and out of my consciousness. I tried to focus. I really did. But all I could see was a dancing dog. After he left us with a pile of information packets and waivers and support group numbers, I walked over to Charlie, who was sleeping peacefully at the moment hugging his green frog pacifier. He couldn't use the thing but loved it anyway and clutched it like a lady does her purse on the subway. I put my hand, gently, on his chest, feeling the rise and fall. I let a finger drift over his neck. How could we ravage such a thing?

Everybody knows the story of Samson. He's the strong man, like Achilles, with gloriously flowing locks of hair. He's Gaston in *Beauty and the Beast*, holding up benches lined with ladies. He's the flexer and the grinner. Samson tore apart lions with his bare hands. He caught three hundred foxes and tied their tails together with torches and set them on the Philistines. He killed a thousand men with the jawbone of a donkey. You just don't mess with Samson . . . unless you're Delilah, but that's another story.

Nobody ever talks about Samson's parents—the ones who raised the little Gaston. It began like most stories of great men in the Bible do: with a barren woman and an angel. Manoah had a wife who was paid a visit by an angel saying, "You are sterile and childless, but you are going to conceive and have a son" (Judges 13:3). He goes on to say this boy will be "a Nazirite, set apart to God from birth, and he will begin the deliverance of Israel from the hands of the Philistines" (Judges 13:5). That's a hefty swig of responsibility for a zygote and his mom. There are certain rules she had to follow along the way. She could drink no wine and eat no unclean food, typical OB orders. But here's the one off: She couldn't cut his hair. No saving that first baby curl for her. When she relayed all this to Manoah, he wanted verification. He needed more details, more clarification, something. If he was going to raise a little Thor, he wanted operating instructions. So he prayed, "O Lord, I beg you, let the man of God you sent to us come again to teach us how to bring up the boy who is to be born" (Judges 13:8).

I was right there with Manoah as Jody and I talked in circles about the tracheotomy. I just wanted someone to show up with a manual and tell me what to do. No one had that crystal ball, not the ENT or the residents who stood like ladies-in-waiting just behind him. No one could say for certain this would end the breathing spells and get us out of the NICU. What if we went through this major surgery and then came out the other side the same or worse? Motherhood, both the getting there and the being there, can send you into the "what if" tailspin. It can make you second-guess every single past and future life choice. But somehow, you have to shake out your worries like a foot that's fallen asleep and get past that miserable tingling, so that you can move again.

In the end, the Lord knew we couldn't make this decision on our own. He had Charlie make it for us. The breathing spells began to increase like contractions, coming closer and closer together and more powerfully. We watched as he lost interest in playing, choosing instead to lie unmoving and watch the musical mobile rotate above him. He let his pacifier roll into a corner of the crib and stay there. He was tired and he was fighting a losing battle. So we signed the waivers and tried to dredge up a little positivity. This could be the end to the nightmarish calls from nurses, of him turning blue, of the screeching alarms and sleepless nights. This could make him safe. This could bring him home.

But no one could have prepared me for the moment my

son was wheeled away by a team of surgeons. This stands out vividly against the blurry outline of all those weeks. They had already switched the ventilator and monitors over to portable machines on his rolling bed. He had ropes of cables and battery packs and oxygen tanks lumped unceremoniously around his crib. He looked at us, calmly, a little resigned, like, *Come on, let's get this over already.* I had been okay, held together with a gossamer thread of anticipation for a better future. But when they began to roll him away, I shattered. Running the few steps to catch up, I grabbed hold of the side of the crib, leaned in around the equipment, and kissed every part of his neck I could reach. Every little sensitive patch of skin I covered with tears and slobber. I was more hysterical now than any other time in our stay. Maybe it was the weight of it all, now falling into place, or the exhaustion, or just the first test of many to see if we had made the right parental decision. Whatever it was, it left me bereft. Jody steered me away as I left pieces of myself, like stray Legos, along the corridor. He took me to the designated "Family Area." This was, as all the veterans knew, with its soft chairs, sunny windows, and ample tissue boxes, the crying room.

Eventually, we went downstairs to the main floor to get the good coffee. I needed something to bring me back to life. We sat hunched over Americanos, praying that God would work a miracle. We prayed the same prayer we prayed through infertility: "Please help us to be good stewards of our own lives and any life you grant us." This is a prayer I still pray. And then we read and reread the manuals for the suction machine that we would have to operate to keep his airway clear. We read the manual on how to change trach tubes, like swapping out tires, because it would have to be done twice a week. We read the instructions on how to safely bathe him so we did not get water down the hole. We studied the diagrams on how to perform infant CPR through the trach. We learned how to position the sticky electrode on his foot that would measure his oxygen levels and heart rate. It made his toe glow like ET's finger. There was so much weight now. So much more than I ever thought I'd have to shoulder as a mom. I had never thought much about this point, the point after the baby comes out. If anyone had asked what I pictured, I probably would have described something out of *Lady and the Tramp*, all pastels and faceless sleeping bundles.

The first glimpse of Charlie post-tracheotomy was grotesque, but comical. Because of the anesthesia and surgery, his face had swelled up like a balloon, like those dolls you win at arcades whose eye bulge when you squeeze them. The trach itself looked huge on his little neck, like a gag bow tie. I wondered how we were ever going to keep his hands off it. It was a built-in toy. What kid wouldn't grab at it? But we wouldn't have to worry about that for at least the next seventy-two hours because Charlie would remain sedated to keep him still so the hole could heal correctly, like a fresh ear piercing that you couldn't remove or fiddle with too much.

I spent those three days at his bedside learning a very different care routine. Along with the temperature checks and diaper changes, I struggled into latex gloves and changed the gauze around the hole site, cleaning with sterile Q-tips and saline solution, and I practiced changing the full trach on a manikin baby of indeterminate sex. I had to apologize to it more than once for dropping it on the floor. I practiced using the battery-powered suction machine that came in a back-pack. It sounded like a lawnmower. Charlie would later grow so used to this sound that he could sleep through it. Unfortunately, the patrons at church never could. We always made sure to sit in the back pew. The sound would become the white noise to our lives. Comforting in its weird way.

Once the immobilization period was over, the true test came. Would Charlie be able to breathe so we could get out of this place? It was a quiet experiment. Because the trach causes air to circumvent the vocal cords, Charlie could no longer make noises. This was, perhaps, the hardest part for me. I would look into his eyes knowing he needed something, but not knowing what. I'd catch myself on the verge of saying, "Speak up!" But there would be no crying or fussing or first words for a long while yet. We had the opposite of a wailing, colicky baby. He would still cry, but it was silent, like a sad mime with tears rolling down his cheeks.

At first the breathing grew worse instead of better. Our ENT had warned us this might happen. Charlie now had to learn to breathe in this new way and he was also weaker after surgery. Those were the days I wanted to beat my fists against my forehead or my forehead against the wall. The head of the English department from my school came to visit me with her teenage daughter on one of those days. Right as the nurses in reception called to tell me she was in the lobby, Charlie had a bad spell and they had to take him out of my arms and administer oxygen. I came out long enough to say hello. The look on my face gave her daughter the best birth control she could ever ask for. Mothering is tough business.

When Manoah asked God how they should raise their

son, he said "teach us" how to do this parenting thing and God replied, "Your wife must do all that I have told her . . . She must do everything I have commanded her" (Judges 13:13–14). Throughout this process, I had convinced myself that Charlie's fate rested on me. I was the one who would be staying home with him and the machines and the monitors and the medical equipment until I could no longer stretch out my leave of absence. I had even purchased clear plastic shoeboxes and dusted off my crafting skills to decorate them with swirls of blue like the ocean and fancy lettering that spelled out EMERGENCY TRACH KIT. My kid's trachs had flair. I thought if I did enough, if I worked hard enough, Charlie would come home. I overprepared in the hopes that God would see my diligence and reward it. I somehow did not think Jody needed to make this kind of effort. I was the mother after all. If I followed the proper steps, all would be well. Hubris has many languages. Motherhood is one.

When Charlie did not immediately improve, I took it personally. The whole thing felt hugely unfair. We had trusted God in making this decision and it seemed like a cheat move to send us back to the point of desperation. When Charlie did finally start to have fewer and fewer episodes and took a bottle and grew stronger than we'd ever seen him, I realized it had nothing to do with me. He just needed time, the one thing I had not wanted to give.

I get the pressure Manoah and his wife must have felt to be given the huge responsibility of Samson. They had rules to follow and a child to protect so that he could grow to become the protector of an entire people. There are times in life when it does all feel like it's on your shoulders to make the impossible

possible. But man, we just make it so much harder on ourselves. We don't usually get an angel to explain the rules, but God does point us in the general direction through prayer and wise friends and experts. After this, though, He leaves a gap in the action to make us trust Him because His plan will be revealed in His own time. You've always got to mind the gap. And when you're in it, you might as well remain in the "Family Room" with all the other people who love you and yours. Your time will come when you are summoned to action, but for now, you must rest and wait and listen for the call.

Guiding Questions

1. When have you been placed in a position, like Samson's mother, with more responsibility than you could handle?
2. How could you let some of that responsibility rest on others and actively trust God with the outcome?
3. When have you seen God work out a situation that you felt was impossible or unsolvable?

Scripture

- Judges 13:1–25

Chapter 21

"The Graduation" and Ruth

New England in July isn't New England in September, when leaves paint the countryside golden, but it will do in a pinch. Back in our baby-making heyday before we knew what a fertility clinic was, we decided to take a vacation, a big hurrah before being saddled down with kids. The initial trip had been for Italy, but was downgraded to stateside because of a snafu, shall we say, on Jody's part. He forgot to confirm the plane reservations we *thought* we'd made six months in advance. We did not discover this user error until a month before we were scheduled to depart, after bed-and-breakfasts had been reserved, and many Saturday afternoons had been spent on bookstore chaises poring over restaurant guides and English-Italian dictionaries. By then the cost to fly abroad was beyond even our pre-IVF budget. But a downgrade to New England wasn't such a sacrifice. Some of my favorite people come from New England: Benjamin Franklin, Stephen King, Amy Poehler.

We lost ourselves for ten days on meandering car rides through winding coastal roads. We walked the Freedom Trail in Boston. We toured the Iron Works shipyard and drank flights of beer in Bath. We biked through empty cranberry bogs and then watched *Casablanca* in bed with tea and cookies in Cape Cod. We ate apple cider donuts at an orchard in New Hampshire and lobster rolls and crab cakes in every state. We hiked through Arcadia National Park and got lost looking for a lighthouse in Maine. It was what you want out of a trip— freedom to wing it. If you watch little kids playing outside for two minutes, you'll know what I mean. They have an uncanny ability to forget themselves in the details: a spiky bug, a broken shell, an old Band-Aid you wish they hadn't touched. Maybe it's their proximity to the ground, but they don't know to worry about the itinerary, the dirt on their shoes, the message on their phone, the work left undone. Maybe that's why grown-ups live for vacations. They offer us the chance to stop time and explore again, to fall into a rhythm more dictated by the sun than the clock. It's what I yearned for during those trying years of "trying" and it's what I want most as a mother, to lead by example and forget the plans, at least a little.

This was what we craved after Charlie's tracheotomy. We wanted to get out of the NICU and into a life not delineated by shift changes and rounds and set feeding schedules. We were weary of wearing wristbands to gain access to our own child. Even the ability to go outside would be novel. It was nearing on summer. Charlie was almost three months old and he'd never been outdoors. We knew our normal would not be like others. We knew we'd be going home with equipment and instructions and emergency numbers, but it would be our normal, our home. We could begin our life.

To get there, Charlie had to pass a few tests. A few more anyway. He had to gain weight. Check. He had to maintain his temperature. Check. He had to eat well. Check, sort of. He still lost a lot out of the side of his mouth and it took forever, but he was eating. He also had to keep breathing, with no blips, for twenty-four hours, even during the mandated car seat test. I don't think I breathed, for fear of jinxing it, while he sat buckled in on the floor of the hospital room. He fell asleep. We were on our way.

I had moved into the NICU for a week to live with Charlie in the special wing designated for those on their way out. This was to train parents before releasing them into the wild, like boot camp. It felt so strange to sleep in the same room with a baby. This was the first time that Charlie and I were "on our own." Jody would come and go with work, but it was just me and the little guy buddying up for the most part. I think I talked more to Charlie in those few days than I've ever spoken in my life. There was so much I wanted to tell him about the world he was going to see so very soon. And he seemed so interested, staring at me with those Precious Moments eyes.

When our time was up and they finally let me ceremoniously unhook him from all the monitors and gently clean the places on his skin where the probes had left sticky red marks, I cried happy tears along with my mom and all the doctors in the room. Everybody was invested in this one. The very first thing I did was walk him over to the window and hold him up so he could see outside, like Simba in *The Lion King*. I have a picture from that moment. I'm looking at him and he's squinting in the bright sunshine, already beginning to acclimate to a less controlled world.

You should have seen our processional to the car. After ten weeks in the NICU, we had a caravan of belongings plus medical equipment and all the freebies (packages of diapers and sterilized water and tiny bottles of Johnson & Johnson shampoo). We marched out in a parade of balloons and stuffed animals with any nurses and residents our doctor could round up. We needed them all to bear witness. With that first step through the sliding glass doors, I felt something relax inside me. Charlie startled and perked up when he felt the warm breeze as we waited for Jody to bring around the car. I could hear the water burbling from the fountain in the Children's Garden next door and the air whooshing softly in and out of Charlie's trach. It was peaceful. It was then that I whispered a prayer of gratitude for this place and for God leading us out of it and home.

When Naomi left Moab after her husband and sons died, Orpah returned to the safety of her family. Ruth, as you know, chose to follow her mother-in-law and leave the familiar. She said, "Don't urge me to leave you or to turn back from you. Where you go I will go, and where you stay I will stay. Your people will be my people and your God will be my God." In case that wasn't proof enough, she added, "May the Lord deal with me, be it ever so severely, if anything but death separates you and me" (Ruth 1:16–17). This must have been some kind of otherworldly mother–daughter-in-law relationship.

As you may recall, Naomi wasn't a peach to be around at this time, an angry Katharine Hepburn in *The African Queen*. Yet Ruth remained. I am sure when Ruth was being courted by and then married to Naomi's son, she did not envision herself a widow and living in a foreign city. Who would? She did not know she would later follow harvesters in the field, begging off scraps for food (Ruth 2:6–7). Or that Naomi would order her to "wash, put on perfume, and get dressed in your best clothes," only to "go down to the threshing floor . . . note the place where [Boaz] is lying . . . uncover his feet and lie down" (Ruth 3:3–4), like a dog at her master's feet. Yet to all this, Ruth's answer was: "I will do whatever you say" (Ruth 3:5). That's the longest trust-fall in history. I would have kicked Naomi in the shins and run away. But it panned out. She married the man and had the child who would one day be the grandfather of King David.

God does not abide by our plans. When Jody and I first starting trying to get pregnant not long before that New England trip, I did not picture the needles, the loss, the sickness, and then the baby who would not come home for months. I did not picture all the gear he would need or the nurse I would need to become. But I also did not picture the look on his face when we first walked outside or the feeling of stepping into our house and taking him on the tour of his room and the yard and introducing him to the dog. I did not picture the heartbreaking gratefulness I would feel when finally cutting that hospital band off my wrist and his. This is what change forces us to do. Like vacations, it pushes us to leave our preconceptions behind and check out what the world's got going for it. Infertility and the early years of motherhood can make you feel like Bill Murray in *Groundhog Day*, every day the same, one long déjà vu. But it *is* changing. It's changing you. It's making you a more compassionate and empathetic human, even if you don't feel it until it has come and gone.

In hindsight, we might have been a little too ambitious that first afternoon. It was a beautiful late May day. The trees were now fully foliaged and proud of it. It wasn't yet humid.

The mosquitos had not hatched. After all the hospital living and hand sanitizing and alcohol swabbing, we wanted some airing out. We needed to smell grass and hear birds and sprinklers and prove to our neighbors that we were still alive. So after unloading the car and making sure Charlie's little foot was hooked up to the monitor, we attempted our first family walk.

With me pushing Charlie, and Jody walking the dog, we set out. We made it fifty yards, at most. We could still see the house when the monitor that had been humming reassuringly fell off the edge of our never-before-used stroller and crashed to the ground. It made one long slow beep and then died. The fall had had that slow-motion quality to it, long and seemingly easy to prevent. My mind stayed three seconds behind the action and then everything flipped into fast forward. Jody tripped over the dog's leash as he lunged to catch it and then took a knee, like a player on the field. We both stared as it lit up again and began flashing random numbers and beeping at odd intervals, a Morse code it dared us to crack. It had been less than two hours since we'd left the hospital and we'd already gummed it up. How did they ever let us out? We clearly needed supervision. Jody ran back to the house to get the manual. Charlie studied the trees from his nest in the stroller, unconcerned.

I noted, in the interim, that his eyes were the exact blue as the shallow end of the pool, clear and a little sparkly. How had I never seen this before? He also had approximately three blond hairs on his head, all of which peeked jauntily out from his green cap. The creases in his ears made him look like a punk rocker, baby Billy Idol. I drank him in. And he eyed me in return, like a shopper sizing up the produce. I straightened my shirt and tried to make a good impression. By the time Jody came back with the manual and reset the machine, we had finished our introductions. We finished the walk with a little more ease. Only the dent at the corner of the monitor would tell the tale.

This was my moment. I had met my son. Most people would see the trach and tongue before they saw Charlie. But on this afternoon, God knew I needed to first learn the lesson I would be called upon to teach others: There's a boy in there and he's offering you the chance to take a vacation from the ordinary. It was yet another extension of the lesson he had been teaching me all along the ravaged road to motherhood.

Expectations are just that—what you expect. They are ideas. God's reality is much richer than that. God will always give you the right version of your life.

Over the course of the next few months, Charlie would be dogged in his mission to remind us that he was, after all, just a kid. We'd wake panicked in the night to alarms blaring, signaling serious distress, and race to his bed, which was only feet away because we were too nervous to actually put him in his fancy nursery at the other end of the house. We'd run, yanking on the sterile gloves, only to find him smiling and sucking on the probe that had been carefully wrapped around his foot. Its red glow lit up his mouth like a Christmas tree. He'd also yank the protective cover off the front of the trach and drown it in drool. He'd turn up his nose at tummy time and sleep with his gauze blanket placed directly over his face, exactly how they tell you not to let your child sleep. My mom accidentally de-trached him while pulling his shirt over his head. Off went the shirt and out went the trach. She almost fainted getting it back in while he laughed his wheezy laugh through the open hole.

I'm certain Ruth had her moments of doubt while she walked the long road back to Bethlehem. No one is immune to indecision or regret. She must have wondered what she was getting herself into when Naomi was brooding or when she spent more time begging for food than eating it. I'm sure she dreamt of home and the familiarity and safety that went along with it. But something propelled her to keep going until she reached a new life.

God makes us mothers to bring us to our knees, to get down in the dirt and see the nature of things. This is the greatest lesson we can learn in life. There is a plan and it is not ours. It is better.

Guiding Questions

1. How has the road to motherhood taught you to view your life plan differently?
2. When have you seen God's plans turn out better than your own?
3. What is one trait God has strengthened in you in this journey?

Scripture

- Ruth 1:16–17, 2:6–7, 3:3–5

Chapter 22

"The Acknowledgment" and Mary at the Wedding

Weddings bring out the best and the worst in people. They cultivate a low-grade mania. It's a heavy atmosphere, watching two people promise to love each other in sickness and in health 'til death. It brings eternity to light, and as you sit in the audience and listen to the promises, that either sounds amazing or disappointing. Your perspective generally stems from the minutiae: whether you were late, if you fought with your spouse in the car, if kids are in attendance, and so on. We're temporal creatures. The imminent is always the biggest winner in the emotional tug-of-war. This is probably why open bars at weddings are a bad idea. You just don't know what side of the car people got out of that day.

Jesus was still at the front end of His preaching when He attended a wedding in Cana with His family and the disciples. They were a close-knit group, more buddies at this point than leader and followers. As is often the case with big weddings or long receptions, they ran out of wine. Back then it was a sign of wealth and respect to throw the biggest and best celebration in town. The party could and should go on for days. We're not sure how far along in the festivities they were when

Mary whispered to her son, "They have no more wine" (John 2:3), but apparently, it was not far enough. No one was calling for their driver just yet.

I always hear His reply, for improbable reasons, in the manner of John Cleese: "Dear woman, why do you involve me?" (John 2:4). He was not ready to draw the attention to Himself that He knew was coming soon, like a traffic jam in the distance. But here's my favorite part: Mary ignored Him. Instead, she turned to the servants and said, "Do whatever he tells you" (John 2:5). She was in mom-mode and took it for granted that Jesus could and would perform this first small miracle. She knew the man He was and she had complete faith in Him, as mothers usually do with their children. And I can't help but love this: He humored her. You know how the story goes. He turned that water into wine and the party rolled on. This was "the first of the signs through which he revealed his glory; and his disciples believed in him" (John 2:11). It was the beginning of the big things, and Mary broke the inaugural champagne, as she had done from the beginning.

Not long ago, we found ourselves at Jody's family reunion in North Carolina. It took place in the gym of a small local church, where aunts and nieces had set up round tables and folding chairs. Fried chicken, green beans, and all the fixings sat in orderly rows on metal tables in the industrial kitchen while kids pinballed through the crowd, throwing balls and hula hoops perilously close to the food and the elderly.

Charlie was now almost five. He was in his wheelchair, but trach free. There was no crystal ball, but if there had been, I would have given thanks early on for this outcome. He was flanked by his younger twin siblings, Jonas and Cora, more hatchlings from our frozen embryos. Twins were not part of the plan, but of course, what in our journey has been? We were par for the course in the unexpected and happier for it. Our kids were wired from unmonitored access to desserts that had followed the incarcerating car ride over from Tennessee. It was loud to the point of hearing loss in the gym. Sounds of scattered conversations and basketball dribbles and tennis shoe squeaks echoed off the walls and lacquered flooring. It was a celebration of family, much like a wedding. It was a ceremony, a gathering of people to show their love and commitment to one another over the years.

For a reason I cannot now remember, maybe the sudden calm, I happened to look up from packing the bags for the long car ride home and spotted Jody and his dad lined up at the far end of the gym. They had Charlie in his wheelchair and the twins and cousins in similar positions on either side, little soldiers awaiting orders. After a few slow and theatrical counts to three, they raced. Children ran, Charlie rolled, Jody slipped and fell, and all the ladies at the other end, including me, clapped. Back and forth, back and forth, they raced until Jody was reduced to a galumphing walk. Jonas and Cora dragged him forward by the shirttails while Charlie signaled them all to march on, pick up the pace, my little conductor. They rolled into me, all the pieces of my life in one sweaty hug out of bounds.

It was a small thing really, hardly a moment to tell. But that's the point. Somehow, through God's grace, I had found myself settled deep down in the groove of life watching my children, whom I had once believed would never exist, race each other. I was suddenly present, in mind and body, how I wished I had been all along this journey to motherhood. I was at the party and Jesus had supplied the wine.

It comes and goes, this present-ness, this letting go. But I try to notice it, like a passing cloud, when it happens along. There's a reason Jesus' first miracle of turning water into wine is such a small one. There is a reason we see Mary take for granted her son's ability to do the miraculous. It's so that we never will.

Having undergone infertility, loss, and all manner of unexpected turnings on the road to motherhood, I try not to assume anything anymore. But it is a hopeful unassuming. My journey resulted in children, and for that I am beyond thankful, even as they make me want to pull the minivan of life over until everybody collects themselves. Life is a continual etching and erasing. We form expectations, and God forms reality. Sometimes they line up nicely, like tracings at right angles. And sometimes God plays Jackson Pollock and we're all over the place. But the point of it all is that a masterpiece is being made.

I pray that no matter what turns your life takes, you try to stay in the present and to acknowledge the woman that you are becoming on this journey, one joined with the rest of the women in the Bible who struggled with their faith and circumstance and came out stronger for it.

Guiding Questions

1. If you could give one piece of advice to another woman about motherhood, what would it be?

Scripture

- John 2:1–12

Acknowledgments

How and where to start? Jody, thank you for marrying me and making me a mother. You are, almost, endlessly patient. Thank you for trying all the spicy foods and bringing me the *New York Times* crossword and breaking all the rules of the McDonald's PlayPlace so Charlie can play too. That's love.

And to Keely Boeving, my agent, this book would still be a really long thought bubble without you. Thank you for seeing the thread of the message and pulling at it until we found its center. And thank you for prodding me into the Internet world of publication so I could write myself out in the interim. And to Keren Baltzer, my editor, thank you for taking a chance and a great deal of long-distance calls to make this come to fruition.

I'd also like to thank Glenn, my reproductive endocrinologist who coaxed my three amazing kids into being. You have a way about you. As do you, Anne, my fearless obstetrician. Thank you for coming in on your night off and sorry about those tennis shoes.

And to my parents, what can I say? You never once doubted I'd make a book into being. Or a being into being. Thank you for always believing. And thank you for the babysitting— thank you most for that.

And to my kids—my Charlie, my Jonas, my Cora. How

many words does it take to tell you what you mean to me? I don't know, but I'm not done yet.

Someone once told me that when it comes to kids, you should always expect the unexpected. It's the same for life, really. It's the necessary wear and tear that breaks it in and makes it livable, like a good couch. Thank you, Jesus, for the wear and tear.

About the Author

Jamie Sumner is a writer for *Parenting Special Needs Magazine* and an editor for *Literary Mama* as well as a regular contributor to *Scary Mommy*, *Mom.me*, *Parent.co*, and other publications. Her IVF journey was also featured on Fox 17 News. She and her husband fought infertility for two years before seeking medical intervention. She has a son, Charlie, diagnosed with Beckwith-Wiedemann syndrome and cerebral palsy, and boy-girl twins, Jonas and Cora. Jamie lives in Nashville, TN, and can be found at www.mom-gene.com.